Write To Meow: 2015

Edited by:
Diana Kathryn Plopa

Grey Wolfe Publishing, LLC
PO Box 1088
Birmingham, Michigan 48009
www.GreyWolfePublishing.com

© 2015 Grey Wolfe Publishing, LLC
Published by Grey Wolfe Publishing, LLC
www.GreyWolfePublishing.com
All Rights Reserved

ISBN: 978-1628281293
Library of Congress Control Number: 2014920014

Grey Wolfe Publishing LLC
Ní bóna na corbín

Write To Meow 2015

Edited by Diana Kathryn Plopa

Dedication

We humbly dedicate this book to the cat; young ones, old ones, and all those in between suffering in shelters, waiting for their "furever" homes.

Perhaps through the writing contained in these pages, more humans will come understand the unconditional love and selfless devotion you bring to our lives, and open their hearts and homes to you.

No more homeless cats, this is our prayer for you today and always!

Acknowledgements

We would like to send out a special **Thank You** to all of the fine authors who submitted their work for this book. It is because of your dedication to cats as well as the writing craft that we have been able to produce such a spectacular tribute to our furry friends!

We also want to thank the good people of **New Beginnings Animal Rescue** who fight tirelessly day after day to make sure that cats find all the love, medical care, and comfort they deserve!

And finally, we want to thank **you**, the person who purchased this book and is about to read it. Because of your interest in cats, or perhaps because of the relationship you have with one of the authors, cats will be saved, cared for, and find a special place in loving homes!

Contents

Thank You, Authors!

We believe in the power of the pen. We believe that literacy is an important part of a successful life. We are committed to saving cats from death row, and we asked for your help. You responded with an enthusiasm we could have never predicted; and we are tremendously grateful!

The goal of this collection is to bring awareness to the plight of the thousands of cats that are currently suffering in shelters and needlessly walked into the gas chamber. 100% of the proceeds from the sale of the *2015 Write To Meow* anthology will support the work of **New Beginnings Animal Rescue**, a no-kill animal haven in Michigan, as they save cats from a fate that is death. Their important work is supported entirely through the generous hearts and hands of people like you.

This book is a collection of poetry, short fiction stories and personal essays about cats. The guidelines were simple: write something that includes a cat as a character, or a no-kill shelter as a locale. We were thrilled to receive such a diverse collection of words that will most certainly make a difference in the life of cats!

The purring voices of the cats you have helped, we hope, will be incentive for you to foster, adopt, donate or perhaps volunteer at a no-kill shelter in your area.

Thank you, again. Your words have made a tremendous difference in the lives of these precious souls!

1.
Amanda
William Doreski

Amanda in her many stripes
curls and exposes her belly,
eager for pets. Her sister,
a shy calico, the beauty
of the family, hunkers
at a water dish, wary of me.
The corridor is too narrow,
but it's home to twenty cats.

Angel lived here, and Gemini.
Angel sneered at everyone.
Gemini, calico angora,
climbed my trouser leg
and slept in the crook of my arm
as I dished out food to the others.
When someone adopted her
my inner organs clenched.   Angel,

also taken, left a fistula
only slightly smaller.   Months
have passed, and Amanda still poses
for the attention she needs.
Vacuuming, dumping litter,
washing and bleaching dishes,
restocking food, towels, water
take time, leaving few moments

for stroking and playing with friends.
Amanda wants to come home with me,
wants her sister to tag along.
When I turn off the lights only
the window at the far end glows
with twilight.   Amanda's eyes flick
silver a moment, then close
as she coils into herself, grieving.

2.
BAD LUCK KITTY
Diane Arrelle

I guess you could say I was having a not-so-good day when the dog charged me. Up until I heard that snarling beast, it hadn't been a really a bad day, just a typical spring day. You know, Sonny woke up with a hangover, told me how sorry he was about last night, then smacked me again for good measure. He said he was sorry... sorry he'd ever married me, sorry he'd ever knocked me up, sorry I was still around to remind him that all his hard earned money was wasted on me and Beth. He was sorry that I'd survived all the beatings, accidents, broken bones and childbirth.

The only saving grace in my life was that Sonny was only a cheap, mean, nasty son of a bitch and not a homicidal one. At least not yet.

Anyway, I was taking a walk in the slightly chilly March air, nursing my bruised cheek and trying to figure out where Sonny hid the money so that Beth and I could take it and run away, when all of a sudden I looked up and saw a black cat with a crooked tail cross my path. "That's just great!" I muttered, then shuddered. "Just what I need some bad luck!"

As if in answer, I heard barking and it was growing nearer. Not the nice kind of barking, but that growling, snarling kind. Then a monstrous dog crashed through the hedge on my left and charged at me. I froze. I read somewhere that you should never run and I now knew why. That's because your legs are suddenly made of jelly and if you try to run you'll only fall and make it easier for the dog to rip out your throat.

So I stood, frozen and waited to die, but the dog suddenly jerked to a stop and I could see it was part pit bull, part mastiff and a big part Swamp Thing. With fangs bared and slobber hanging in long, dirty strings of drool, the dog stared off to my right and suddenly took off past me.

To say I was surprised was an understatement! I looked back at the charging hellhound and saw him running down that black cat. *Poor kitty,* I thought and felt a surge of relief as the cat headed for a tree and was up it in a second, leaving the dog running in circles around it yammering like crazy. "Thanks kitty, seems you have the bad luck now," I whispered then slowly walked away leaving the two animals to work out their problems. I felt bad for the cat, but he was safe in the tree and maybe the dog would just circle the tree until he melted into a pool of butter.

Back home, I noticed Sonny's motorcycle was gone so I tiptoed into the garage and looked for the hiding place. Sonny didn't like banks; he just hid our money to be safe. Only it wasn't really our money, it was mine. It was my insurance settlement for the roof after that tornado. The house was still in my name, belonged to my parents before they died. But Sonny, he took the money and fixed the roof himself. I know he stole the supplies from the roofing company he'd been fired from. And from the way the back room leaked, I know why they canned him. And then there's the money from the accident, the one where he was driving drunk but ran away before the cops showed up. Since the other driver in the other car died, Sonny sued the estate for all my pain and suffering. After all, it was a head-on and we were on the correct side of the road, except that the other driver had swerved to miss Sonny who was on the wrong side and then he suddenly jerked the wheel to cross the line smashing us into the other car. Sometimes I wonder if he did it on purpose to kill me. Too bad I never saw any of that money either.

I heard a sound and stiffened. I didn't want Sonny to see me snooping around so I turned and went back outside. There was that black cat again. Strutting in front of me, acting like he forgave me for abandoning him after he saved my bacon. He strolled over and wove his way between my legs back and forth and I could hear him purring like Sonny's bike on idle.

Glancing around to make sure Sonny was out wherever it is he disappears; I stooped and picked the cat up. He fit perfectly in my arms and still purring he butted my chin affectionately with his head. I scratched him behind his ears and smiled. Few things make me smile anymore. Seeing my little girl laugh could always make me smile, but Beth hardly laughed anymore. She just kind of skulks around the house trying to act invisible whenever her daddy graced us with his presence.

"Poor kitty cat," I said burying my face in the cat's soft dark fur. "You're just a bad luck kitty. If Sonny sees you, you won't have enough lives to survive. He's one superstitious man!" I shuddered and remembered how he had broken a mirror and given me seven years of bad luck. Old Sonny never walked under a ladder or opened an umbrella in the house. Man, if he saw this black cat it could scare him to death. Thinking that thought, I realized I'd finally found another thing that could make me smile.

I put the cat down and went inside to fill a bowl with milk. I'd feed him far away from the house so Sonny wouldn't find him and kill him. I finally had a friend and I wasn't about to lose him to that maniac I'd unfortunately married.

I took the bowl out and frowned. My new friend was nowhere to be seen. Leaving the back door ajar, I wandered the neighborhood calling, "Here kitty, here cat."

I felt like crying when I realized he had split. *Just like a man*, I thought with a bitter laugh. *Love em and leave em*. Then I really laughed, laughed so hard I started to cry. If only Sonny had followed that old adage, I'd be a happy woman today. "Someday I'm going to find that money then it's good-bye bastard."

I returned home, went in the slightly opened door and felt panic clawing at my throat. This day was just getting worse and worse. The cat had somehow gotten inside and walked in the fireplace then on the carpet. I saw the trail of dark gray footprints and wanted to scream. How was I going to clean this up before Sonny returned? He'd see the prints and beat me for sure. Then I noticed the prints led from the fireplace to a pile of logs on the floor. Sonny warned me to leave them alone when I cleaned. "You never know when I'm going to want to make a fire," he said. "So don't mess with my wood unless you want to cut down a tree and lug it in here yourself."

I always figured that the firewood in the corner was just another of Sonny's quirks. He had a lot of quirks. I once moved them looking for the money, but he saw they'd been rearranged and hit me. I never touched them again. But now the cat was sitting on one log with his tail twitching. "Rouwull," the cat growled and pawed at the side of the wood.

I walked over to him following his footprints and stared at the log. It looked normal enough but then the cat pawed it a little harder and it rolled off the pile.

How could a cat swat a heavy log off the woodpile, I wondered and stooped to pick it up. It was light, like it had been hollowed out. I took it outside and studied it. One end was false like a plug in a bottle. I pried it opened. It was full of money! Not all the money but a good two grand.

"Well kitty," I said going inside and picking up the cat. "You seem to be my hero. Somehow, I'm going to have to figure out a way to keep you. If only you could show me where the rest of the money is hidden."

"Meow," the cat exclaimed and started to purr. I gave him a hug and to my surprise he leapt from my arms and ran out the still opened back door.

I dashed out after him, yelling, "Come back!" But he was history.

Annoyed and hurt, I shrugged then picked up the log and put it back together enough so that Sonny wouldn't realize it was tampered with. I stuck it back on the pile. It looked fine to me. Then I sat in the kitchen and counted my money. Nineteen hundred dollars, yep, it was the roof money. What I needed to find was the insurance settlement. That was the real money.

I glanced at the clock and realized the carpet was still soiled with cat prints. I'd been so preoccupied with the money I'd forgotten to vacuum. Beth would be home soon and I went out to meet the bus hoping Sonny'd stay out another hour and give me time to clean up.

To my surprise a patrol car was pulling into my driveway. *What trouble did Sonny get into this time*, I wondered with a huge resigned sigh. Maybe, if he needed to be bailed out he'd tell me where he'd hidden the rest of the money. Wouldn't that be great!

Instead, two officers came up to me and gently led me back inside. Then they broke the news. Sonny'd had an accident while apparently on his way home. He'd been drinking and... and according to witnesses had swerved off the road to avoid hitting a black cat. He'd died instantly.

The officers stood waiting for my response, the hysterics. I sat stunned. Finally I managed to speak. "Oh my God, did the cat have a crooked tail? He didn't hit it, did he?"

That night after the cops left and the arrangements for the cremation were made, I went outside to put out another dish of milk and a plate of tuna. I wasn't disappointed. My cat sat on the back stoop waiting. He ran over to his well-earned dinner and gobbled it up, then sat at the door as if waiting to be let in. I opened it and he entered like the new king of the house. Maybe he'll help me find the rest of my money, but there was no rush anymore. Sonny had been insured.

"Thank you, kitty," I told him and picked him up.

"I guess it would be tacky to call you Lucky," I added hugging my cat.

But I did anyway and he was.

3.
Dear Billy The Cat
Stephen J. Regan

I remain your servant though I no longer live with you and you no longer rest on my lap. I even miss seeing your arse – and you certainly liked to point it my way very often. Even in my face. I didn't mind that, Billy. I realize that cat manners are different to human ones.

And I miss your nightly soft-paw up my chest and the touch of your nose to my temple. They made my bedtimes complete.

I suspect my ex-girlfriend always wanted you to do the same to her, in which case she should have kept her hands to herself and let you pad your own way, in your own time, across the territory of her body, and without all the excessive stroking and silly squeals (hers, that is, nor yours).

But will you just listen to me! I'm hardly an expert on what made my former lover happy. She said she loved you and that's why she grew to resent me – for being so popular with you. Well, I can't help it. I know intuitively that cats need to be in charge when it comes to physical contact with humans. You clearly loved that I didn't tickle your tummy or fiddle with you tail-end, Billy, in the way that she did. She just can't help herself. Her hands demand regular contact with male tummies and tails.

I mean, she was all over Ryan from sales, in similar fashion, at the office party last Christmas. Oh, I'm not complaining. I liked it well enough when she did that to me in the early stages of our relationship. Looking back, she probably wishes I'd been touchy-touchy and nose-rubby with her, rather like you were, with me, Billy, though she really didn't like that.

Ah well, I've always been good with animals; just rubbish with women!

And you were her cat, after all; she'd possessed you for three years before she even met me. From our second date she made it plain that I needed to get on with her beloved Billy. Never a problem. I was just cool with you, because that's what hep cats such as you prefer, Billy, isn't it?

And now I no longer share a house with you, I miss you very much Billy – much more than I miss her. And here's the deal, I'm prepared to woo her again, seriously, if it means I can move back into the house, and you can sit on my lap again when I'm watching Not Going Out, while not touching you but feeling you breathe; feeling the special connection between man and cat.

That's what I was trying to ask you last week, Billy, as I stood outside her house and stared up to the wide windowsill, where you patrolled like a restless Roman legionary on the walls of Chester nearly two millennia ago. Let's get back together, Billy.

Oh, listen to me! I've been outside her house on the pitiless pavement, looking up and talking to her cat. It has come to that.

I want you back, Billy. It's why I've returned here today; why I'm again looking up at you, imploring, with no regard for my personal dignity. But now you're turning your green orbs away. Oh, no indifference is quite as powerful as the feline version, and I'm feeling your aversion to what used to be.

Maybe you know that a reunion wouldn't work in this house now, not even if I won my girlfriend back, and I don't even want that.

I just want YOU back, Billy the cat.   So I'll have to work out some other plan …

Maybe we could just sail away, you and I, without anything obvious to make our elopement seem silly – such as a pea-green boat or an elegant fowl of an owl playing a small guitar.

Stephen J.   Regan is a poet, playwright and journalist.   His poems *Affirmation* and *No Give Way* are published in *Envoi (October 2014).*   His poems have also appeared in: *Best of Manchester Poets anthology (2011)*; T*he US Literary Journal, Killing the Angel (2014); and Reach Poetry (2013 and 2014).*

Stephen's poem *Unpleasant Valley Sunday* won Runner-up Prize in the *Sefton Arts Writing Competition (2011).*   His poem *Red-bricked* is part of a permanent art exhibition at Wigan North West railway station in Lancashire.   His work also featured in the e-zines of *The Screech Owl* and *The Passionate Transitory.*   He is founder of *The Liver Bards* poetry group in Liverpool.

His play *Tim* – about the bombing of Warrington in 1993 – was performed as part of the *Wirral Festival of Firsts* in July 2014.

An experienced newspaper journalist, Stephen created and published *Partners* – a daily fiction serial in *Today* newspaper, 1990-91.   He also created (and wrote from 1990 to 2001) the UK national TV review column *Sam Brady: the man they can't gag* for *ORACLE* and later for the ITV Teletext services.

Stephen is currently writing two novels – *Bad News for Butterflies* (about office life, love and bickering poets), and *The Wearons* (about extraterrestrials living in Liverpool).

4.
Goodbye to Gloria
William Doreski

"Say goodbye to Gloria,"
the Post-Um note requests. Cancer
has smudged her palate, loosened
her teeth. Soon she won't eat,
so the vet will kill her today
and Laura will freeze her corpse.
Gloria's fluffy gray outlook
narrows to a vanishing point.

Her perch atop the cages
grows precarious. The sloped
light through the one large window
opalesces prismatically, a last
glimpse of the neighboring beyond.
Angelo, her beloved, nuzzles,
unaware of the plot against her.
Bad enough that Kobe left

for San Francisco, clinging
to his adopter with a grin.
Bad enough that Tippy has left
for a house with a friendly dog.
So many have come and gone.
The room dims as the noon sun wanes.
The caged cats hide in dark corners.
They envy the cats loose in the room.

They have never heard of cancer,
don't know that prolonged diets
of dry food kill.   Gloria knows
that something alien inhabits
her mouth.   She tries to explain
to Angelo that she's uneasy;
but he believes that cuddling close
solves even the deepest cruelty.

5.
Grayson's Journey
Alice Woodrome

You might say that I'm the suspicious type. I have my reasons. I started out as naive as any other kitten: snuggled close to my mother with my squirming brothers and sisters all around. Life was easy. When I was hungry I had only to find Mother's swollen teats. She kept me safe and warm and I wanted nothing that she did not supply.

Even when we got old enough to venture away from our tattered blue blanket, we were always within our mother's protective circle. I took the comforts of home and our mother for granted. Life was grand as we played together, rolling green beetles across the dusty floor of the toolshed, stalking wooly worms and garden spiders in the patch of cool grass that was our larger world. So many intriguing scents to investigate. If the bark of a dog or a sudden movement frightened one of us, there was always a home to scurry to, and the comforting attentions of our mother.

I liked the people who lived in the house nearby. They held me gently and murmured soft noises as they stroked my fur, rubbing me under my chin and along my cheeks. It was no wonder I believed all people were kind.

One late afternoon, sun streamed into the shed through cracks in the wall boards and found its way into our cardboard box. My belly was full, and I lay relaxing alongside my six brothers and sisters. I'd had a busy day of exploring and playing with Buddy, my closest sibling. We were ready for our grooming session before we napped.

Mother had begun to clean Scout's face. He closed his eyes and blissfully submitted, while I squeezed past Buddy and Millie in hopes of being next.

The door creaked open. I stretched up to see out of our box. On the threshold stood a man, silhouetted against the open doorway. I'd seen him from a distance most mornings when he got into a white truck that carried him away for the day.

The man took three heavy steps and loomed over us. He smelled like smoke, not like the people who came every day. We cowered as he grabbed Mother out of our box with a large bony hand and dropped her onto the floor. Creamy white Angel scrambled out to follow her. Mother meowed with her whiskers pulled back as the man snatched our sister and dropped her back in with the rest of us. He picked up our cardboard box and carried us outside into the glaring light. Looking through a hole in the box, I watched Mother follow with her tail lashing. She yowled as the man took us across the grass and shoved our box into the back of the truck, where a biting odor made my nose crinkle. I heard her howl as the man climbed into the front and slammed the door shut.

We rumbled along on a scary ride with the air rushing over the top of our box. Scout and I tried to look out a few times, but all I saw was a confusing blur. The fleeting smells were baffling. Angel and Goldie meowed for Mother nearly the whole way. They weren't the only ones worried.

When the noisy ride jerked to an end, I stumbled to my feet, dizzy, with my heart pounding. I heard a door open and close, then the man picked up our box and carried us down a rocky slope. I pulled myself up to see where we were and almost fell out when the man lost his footing. He shouted as he and our box dropped together, hitting the ground with a thud. Goldie started wailing so loud I couldn't think. The man pushed our box with his foot to a level place in the prairie grass. He reached down with his hand and touched Buddy, who shrank and flattened his ears. Scout hissed. The man hurried back up the hill toward the truck. A roar came from the road—and grew fainter until it disappeared. We were alone.

My brothers and I huddled next to our sisters and waited for our mother to find us. The familiar scents of leafy growth were intensified and mixed with strange earthy odors, raw and woodsy. Goldie ceased her loud protests and nestled next to her twin, Golda, mewing softly. Millie didn't settle down until Angel started to lick her. I stayed close to Buddy and stiffened at every noise, hopeful that Mother was near. Scout stretched up now and then to get a better view, but I was glad he stayed with us. Mother would want us together when she came.

When the sky darkened, and she still hadn't arrived, we pressed closer to each other. Sleep came in snatches. We startled at every noise in the black countryside. Goldie and Millie cried when a strange chorus of coyotes howling and yipping reverberated in the distance. A sharp screech that pierced the night air frightened me the most, and I burrowed under the blanket, shuddering with Buddy trembling beside me. Scout was restless, moving around all night. I tried to be brave, but I was cold and hungry—no soft stomach to knead, no sweet milk to suckle. Our only comfort was the warmth of each other's bodies and our mother's scent that lingered on the blue blanket.

Scout was the first to jump out of the box the next morning. Hunger and thirst forced the rest of us out too. We had been left at the edge of a large meadow with patches of sunflowers and a few trees. A breeze, charged with a mix of curious scents, swept over us. A fence row bordered the far end of the meadow. Beyond the fence, a green field extended in lines to a row of trees in the distance—so far away they looked tiny. The blue sky stretched in a vast canopy over it all. A bird sang now and again, and soft lowing drifted from a far off pasture, but mostly there was stillness, so unlike the busy noises of home. Our world had been turned upside-down, and nothing was as it should be.

My insides growled. Mother was nowhere. We searched the prairie grass surrounding the box for something to eat, but found little. I chased a green lizard that ran too fast and a mouse that disappeared down a hole. I caught a couple of crickets and a caterpillar. They didn't taste anything like our mother's milk, and there wasn't enough to make the hunger go away. Instead of the fresh water of home, we drank from puddles. The first time I crouched to lap the water, the reflection of a hawk soaring overhead appeared. Its raspy scream sent a rush of fear all the way to the end of my tail, and I ran to hide under a leafy vine. When the sun sank behind the trees and the sky darkened, we returned to the box, to the warmth and solace we found together.

But how we missed our beautiful mother. Clear green eyes and a silky coat the color of goldenrod. Mother's warm stomach was the most blissful spot imaginable—that deep rumbling purr when I lay next to her, the homey aroma of her breath as she cleaned me. She made me feel loved.

By the time the second long night passed, I knew—as surely as her scent on the blue blanket was fading—I would never see my mother again.

Some of my sisters were slow to accept that we would not be reunited with Mother. By our fourth day in the prairie, they still looked up the rocky hill as if expecting the white truck to return and take us back to her. When we heard thunder on the road above, Goldie always scrambled up the slope first, followed closely by Golda, her constant companion. Millie usually trailed behind.

A car rumbled on the road while I stalked a spotted lizard. My sisters rushed up the slope. I inched closer to the lizard, my whiskers tense. In the distance, another car roared by. Then I heard it: Millie's scream. I rushed back and up the rocky bank. Buddy, Scout and Angel had already gotten there. Our golden sisters lay in the road, their blood mixing as it pooled between them. Golda moved her legs one last time like she was dream-running, then lay motionless beside her beloved sister.

Stunned into silence, we stood looking at them, shocked, bewildered. They lay silent and still, eyes open and mouths, agape. Were they sleeping? Their eyes looked so different, like they saw nothing. I pawed at my sisters, nuzzled them, trying to wake them. Something about them reminded me of the mice our mother caught, so quiet, so limp. Was this the same? Were they asleep forever? Could this be death? I had never considered such a thing—that we might come to the same end as the birds and mice Mother brought home. I tried to awaken them again, meowing. I couldn't believe their life had left them. Buddy and Scout turned sadly and crept back down the slope. Hesitant to leave, I tarried—confused, not believing it, not wanting to. But when I could not rouse our golden sisters, I had to accept it. The twins, lying together in death, the way they had in life, would never awaken. A sickening odor permeated the area.

Little Millie, with dark eyes and drooping ears, crouched low beside their bodies with Angel, meowing softly, next to her. When Millie finally found her voice, an anguished cry resounded across the prairie.

I finally turned to leave the cruel road, slinking low to the ground. I looked back at Millie and Angel, meowing for them to come. They reluctantly followed down the hill, but Millie stopped at the bottom and looked back for a long time. I didn't go up to the road again. Neither did the others. The road smelled of death, and became a hateful place.

Later that day, two enormous vultures swooped down out of the sky and landed where our sisters' bodies lay. Black with naked heads the color of blood, the birds huddled around with shoulders hunched as if conspiring to do something terrible. They lingered a long time, heads bobbing, flying up briefly every time another car rumbled by. My insides hurt when I thought about what might be going on up there.

The death of our golden sisters cast a dreadful pall over us all. Millie wandered about aimlessly for hours, wailing softly. The only time she appeared aware of what went on around her was when another car approached. She cowered in the tall grass until the thunder faded. Angel stayed close to her, but Millie would not settle down. She ate nothing the rest of the afternoon. Later that evening when she was too weary to walk, I brought her a cricket. She looked at it with dull eyes, then lay her head down again and mewed sadly.

That evening we all retreated to the cardboard box before the sky turned dark. Angel licked Millie until she drifted off to sleep. Scout, Buddy, and I cuddled together next to the girls. Though the air wasn't cold, I couldn't stop shivering as I tried to remember what it was like to not be afraid. That night remained mercifully quiet, with just the sound of crickets to lull us to sleep.

I woke at first light. The sky glowed with streaks of pink above the trees. The practical matter of survival required us to leave the comfort of the box, but we did not wander far from each other. Buddy led the way. When Millie lagged, I waited. We spent the morning looking for something to fill our bellies. Butterflies and beetles flew about, too fast to catch. I captured one cricket and a big brown spider; the others did no better. Even Millie knew she needed to eat and tried to catch a grasshopper but finally found a slow caterpillar. When Buddy spotted a little ground mouse, he took chase, and we all tried to keep up. Bigger and faster than we, he was far ahead when he leaped and turned back triumphantly with the mouse in his mouth.

The moment of elation turned to terror when an enormous hawk with talons outstretched dove from the clouds, attacking Buddy. He screamed and released the mouse. Scout arched his back and yowled. As the mouse scurried away, I ran toward my brother who was in the clutches of the monster bird. A violent struggle was over in a moment when the hawk tore at Buddy with its claws. My brother's body went limp and lifeless. I froze. The monster hawk stared at me, its yellow eyes shooting a tremor through my spine. I hissed, shrank, and tucked my tail as the bird flapped its wings and took flight, clutching my brother. Horrified, I watched it ascend directly over me into the sky, Buddy's body dangling beneath. My heart raced and I began to shake as the hawk flew across the road. I wanted to chase after it—kill it or die trying, but it disappeared behind the trees.

Millie retreated further into her own thoughts, and curled up in the grass for a long time that afternoon. Scout threw himself into hunting with a vengeance, and caught enough bugs for everyone.

That night, my misery deepened into torment. Buddy's scream echoed in my mind as coyotes laughed at me in the distance. I didn't sleep. My best friend was gone, and the wild prairie seemed to be making sport of me. Angel licked me repeatedly, but her sweet attentions could not console me.

Rain started falling before sunrise. By morning we were soaked. Our box was reduced to a soggy mound of wet cardboard. Scout and I dragged our blue blanket to a sheltered spot under the branches of a cedar tree. By evening, our bedding had dried—a small matter, but we snuggled into it, grateful for the one thing we still had from home.

We lived on grasshoppers and crickets for days, venturing farther from our tree as hunger compelled us to search for better hunting. When squeaks drifted from the far corner of our meadow, Scout and I cautiously investigated and smelled a strong musky odor as we got closer. We discovered a cluster of sizable holes, the homes of prairie dogs. Too hefty to chase and eat, but at least they didn't chase us. Plenty of bugs lived along the tall grass in the fence row close to their burrows, and we went there often. With experience, we gradually became better hunters. Lizards became a regular part of our diet.

Angel became the first to provide a mouse. She caught it by mimicking the slow motion crawl and lightning-fast attack we had seen our mother employ. We all practiced. Scout became an expert, and even little Millie eventually succeeded.

Constantly on guard, we watched the skies for hawks, and scanned the horizon for foxes and coyotes. The sounds at night still frightened us, but over the course of a few weeks, as we grew bigger and faster, we learned to survive in that harsh place. We were no longer little kittens.

We found some respite in occasional moments of wonder, like the day orange butterflies dotted the sky. They fluttered everywhere. We made a game of jumping at them, batting the air. Sometimes we paused from our constant search for food to watch long lines of geese flying overhead, calling out as they flapped their wings. Or the spectacle of several strong-smelling deer that came to graze along the fence line. One day a dazzling cloud of blackbirds descended on the meadow not far from us as we looked on with wide eyes. After a moment or two, the flock lifted and swirled, its shape twisting wildly until at last, the birds drifted off into the distance.

We caught plenty of mice for a few days when a man on a tractor came to break up the soil in the field beyond our meadow. He turned up the mice burrows as he roared along, releasing a pleasant loamy scent. We caught five the first day, and more the next—much more than we could eat. Scout met with the most success by crouching close to the tractor's path until it stormed by and flushed a mouse. He would pounce on the disoriented creature, then strut as he carried it home to toy with under the cedar branches before we feasted. The man on the tractor wore a cap, like the one worn by the man who took us away from our mother. Too suspicious to get close, I didn't catch nearly as many mice as Scout.

The last afternoon the man plowed, Scout still hadn't returned long after the soil had all been broken and the tractor had gone. My gut knotted. Why was our brother delayed? Unable to rest, I left Millie and Angel and went to look for him. I hurried to the area of the field where I had last seen the tractor. Meowing loudly for Scout, I searched the rows of turned earth. In one of the furrows, I saw something. I stiffened, almost too afraid to look closer. My brave brother lay on the clumpy soil, blood staining his white face. Flies buzzed around him. I backed off, my insides sick. After a few moments, I crept next to Scout's lifeless body. Crouching down with closed eyes, I wrapped my tail around me and stayed for a long time. Both my brothers were gone. I wanted it to be over, all the struggle, the fear—the death and sorrow. But my two sisters needed me. Before it got too dark, I started back to the cedar with my tail drooping. When I came alone, Angel and Millie hung their heads. Angel rubbed the full length of her body against mine and licked my face. We curled up together with Millie, sharing a heavy silence—and didn't sleep.

Between the lizards and mice caught on good days and slow brown grasshoppers, we managed to fill our empty bellies. When the days got shorter and colder, and the mice and bugs scarce, we scratched the soil in search of grubs.

I remember my first snowfall because of Millie. That day we woke to a thin layer of white powder that covered everything, including us. We shook the snow off in wonder then left our blanket to chase the falling white flakes. It was good to be carefree for a while.

A hound's bark broke the spell. A man, walking at the edge of our meadow, followed a reddish dog, bounding through the snow. I looked around for Angel and Millie and spotted them, playing in a drift—too near the dog. Angel, inconspicuous against the whiteness, romped in the snow not far from Millie, whose gray coat stood out. The hound saw her too. I yowled as loudly as I could to divert the dog's attention and to warn my sisters, but it was no use. Millie raced across the field with the dog gaining on her and the man running behind shouting after his hound. Angel raced back to our cedar tree and scrambled up into one of the lower limbs. I ran toward the man and dog but realized before I got very far that I was not fast enough and no match against them anyway. The barking continued after the man and dog disappeared into the trees. I climbed into our cedar to be with Angel and looked toward the woodland, hoping that Millie had found a safe place before the dog reached her. After a few minutes, the man came back into the open tugging the hound by a leash. The dog clearly wanted to resume the chase.

I watched for Millie, hopeful at first that she had managed to escape, but when she didn't come back right away, I knew it wasn't good. Angel was shattered and wandered around meowing the rest of the morning, her tail dragging in the snow. That afternoon I went to look for Millie, expecting to find her body like Scout's. After crossing our meadow, I proceeded through the fence row toward the plowed field where I saw her last. My heart quickened when I heard Millie's pitiful meow. She limped toward me down one of the furrows. I raced to join her.

One look at her dirty fur and mangled paw, and the strong musky odor, told the story. Millie had escaped by diving into one of the prairie dog holes. Either the hound or the inhabitant of the burrow bit her paw in the fray, leaving a serious injury. Shaken and trembling, she whimpered in pain.

Desperately in need of a break, she closed her eyes and leaned into my tongue as I groomed her. When we continued, it was at Millie's pace, only resting when her pain became unbearable. It took the remainder of the afternoon to cross the meadow.

When we returned, Angel ran to meet us, bright eyes and tail held high. Milly settled down on our blanket under the cedar branches. Angel took her turn grooming our little sister. I went to find something for us to eat while Millie lay exhausted next to Angel, purring. Later that evening, we shared a mouse. Even the wintry night did not seem harsh. We had our Millie back.

During the next few days, the snow melted under cloudless skies, but Millie's wound became swollen. Angel hardly left her side. Our sister's trembling body felt hot as I tried to comfort her by cuddling. She cried in pain for so long; it might have been easier for her if the hound had caught her. Angel seemed to be in nearly as much distress as Millie, crying when her sister did.

One late afternoon, after barely moving for days, Millie stirred and tried to crawl but hesitated when Angel licked her face and lay in front of her, their faces touching. I joined my sisters and pawed Millie's foot gently. She opened her eyes for a moment and looked at us, then licked Angel's face just once before struggling to rise again. I knew what she meant. Her time had come, and it was something she had to do alone. When she crawled toward a clump of grass, we did not follow. She huddled down there and returned to her slumber. Our sweet little sister died that afternoon. When we went to check on her, Angel did not want to leave Millie, even when her body grew cold. When it started to snow that evening, she reluctantly joined me back on our blanket. Snow fell all night and buried Millie's body under a thick white mantle.

Then it was just Angel and I. We curled together that night, and I searched for solace in the memories of life in the toolshed. Our mother's warm milk and tender affections. The fun of playing in the green grass with my brothers and sisters. And how soothing it felt to have my fur stroked. The memories didn't help. They only reminded me of how far away that joyful life was from the misery that had befallen us. Even the pathetic blanket Angel and I lay upon testified to the bitterness of our lives now. The fabric, once blue and blissfully soft, had stiffened and faded to gray.

I tried to pretend we'd seen the last of the hard days. But when the snow melted, a biting wind took its place. Every day blew colder than the previous.   No lizards anywhere in the dry grass.   Even grubs were hard to find.

Angel walked around with her head down and tail dragging. She'd lost interest in looking for food and spent most of the time lying under the cedar tree.   Death lingered in the cold air.

Over the next few days our sad situation took a terrible toll. The spark of life faded from Angel's blue eyes.   I licked her the way she had groomed the rest of us so often, but my efforts to console her did not seem to help.   She grew thin and rarely left our blanket and eventually became so weak she could barely walk.   Angel hardly took a bite when I shared my paltry catches with her.   At night I lay close to her to keep her warm, but the only solace she found came wrapped in the shabby blanket.   When she slowly kneaded it as she slumbered, I knew where her dreams were: I still missed our mother too.

Angel seemed farther away from me every day.   When I meowed, she didn't appear to hear me.   When I snuggled next to her, she didn't seem to notice.   Angel stopped eating altogether.   I feared what lay ahead.   Would her life fade away one day like Millie's had?   I wasn't ready when Angel did not awaken one morning.

I nosed her, pawed at her, trying to provoke any response. Her warmth ebbed away, so I pressed close to give her mine.   My sister was all I had left.   All I lived for.   I couldn't allow myself to believe Angel was dead, too.   But her body grew stiff and icy, and I had to accept that she was gone.   I lay alongside her and let the bitterness wash over me.   How had it come to this?   My whole family, everyone I loved—gone forever.   I was alone, really alone.

All goodness had perished.   Only wickedness remained. Nothing and no one could be trusted now.   A part of me wanted to stay beside Angel's still body and never get up.   But my body struggled against my mind.   My aching limbs and rumbling gut refused to surrender. Before the morning passed, I left Angel's cold body on the ashen blanket under the cedar branches and set out on my own.

I walked away from the brown grassland, glancing back only once. I fixed my eyes on the trees in the distance where the sun disappeared every day. Squeezing through the brush that grew along the fence bordering the familiar field, I continued toward the line of timber. Farther than I had ever been. I wanted to get far away from the cruel road that brought us to such a wretched place.

A strong headwind battered me as I trekked along a furrow in the barren field. Wet snow began to fall. It stuck to my fur and paws and made walking difficult. I had to stop regularly to clear the snow packed between my pads. My tongue burned and my nose grew numb. As I pushed toward the trees, memories shuffled through my mind. The man who snatched us from our mother and abandoned us in that bleak prairie. The man who killed Scout when he plowed the field. And the one whose hound chased down Millie. Man was my enemy as surely as the monster bird that took my brother.

As the trees rose before me, my toes and ears became increasingly icy. Surely something on the other side would promise an easier life. Something better than the hunger, the fear, and death I'd left behind.

My belly growled and my body shook when I reached the trees. Relieved to be out of the brutal wind, I lingered for a while in the shelter of the bushy undergrowth.

Two gray coyotes came out of the trees and yelped as they ran toward me. They were almost on me when I turned to run, the sound filling my ears. Any moment I expected to feel their jaws. I spotted a hole and dashed for it, every muscle burning. Splinters scraped my cheek, yanking out a whisker, as I scrambled through the entrance—into a long hollow log. My heart raced as I turned.

One of the coyotes looked in at me with bared yellow teeth, pawing at the decaying wood. Then scratching came from the other end of the log. I couldn't stop panting, my sides heaving, as the coyotes tried to get at me from both ends. The yelping continued sporadically the rest of the day and into the night. I crouched down, trembling as I breathed in the musty smell. Waiting.

The night stretched into an endless ordeal, with strange sounds I never heard in the prairie. The hooting of an owl, the creaking of limbs in the wind, chittering and fluttering in the trees. Peculiar cries sent shivers through me in the darkness. Everything seemed alive and awake around me, and sleep was impossible.

At dawn, the stench of a coyote's breath filled the log. I turned to see eyes glowing at me in the dim light. But the animal could do no more than thrust his head into the end of the log. I was safe. The waiting was not all bad, for when daylight filtered through the trees, and I considered my circumstances, I relaxed in the realization that they couldn't hurt me. Though not warm, the log provided protection from the cold wind, and I found food. A sluggish brown lizard buried in a crevice of the rotting wood and several bugs.

For a brief time, I considered making the hollow log my new home, but as I waited in the dank for the coyotes to leave, a longing began to grow—too hazy to identify. I ached for something more than enough food—more than shelter from the elements. The yearning was for something akin to family, and I wasn't going to find it alone in a hollow log.

A good part of the next day passed before the coyotes gave up. When I hadn't heard or seen them for some time, I stuck my head out and looked around. After a few anxious steps away from the safety of the hollow log, I pressed on through the woods, ever watchful.

The snow had stopped, but the wind still blew strong when I got to the edge of the woods. My body and spirit drooped at the sight of what lay before me: another snow-covered field like the one I had already crossed. Nothing to do but keep going, through that field and then another.

It grew colder every hour. I couldn't see the sun through the clouds and lost track of my direction, but I pressed on. I dreamed of the shed where I was born but dared not hope for anything more than a temporary refuge from the cold and better hunting prospects. When I could go no farther, I happened upon the hollow carcass of a rabbit, ripped apart and stripped of meat. A few morsels were left on the bones. Not enough to satisfy, but enough to give me strength to continue.

The sun, diffused by a layer of clouds, sank toward the treetops and would soon disappear. I couldn't go much farther before finding a place to spend the night. No hope of reaching the woods before the sky darkened. Not a bale of hay or fence post in sight; not even a clump of grass to shield me from the wind. When the light failed, I scratched down in the snow with shaking legs, tucked my nose into my underside, and huddled in a deep furrow. Another cold night, hungry and weak.

A fresh layer of snow covered me when I awoke. Shaking it off, I arched my back, stretched to my full length, and looked across the white field to the trees beyond. The line of timber looked so much like others I crossed. Was I walking in circles?

I trudged toward the trees with half-closed eyes through snow up to my belly. Progress was painfully slow. My energy and spirits slipped away with the frigid wind stinging my face. When I reached the timber, I heard the screech of a hawk soaring overhead, reminding me of Buddy's death. I shuddered and hurried into the shelter of the underbrush.

Resting in the brambles, I tried to gather my strength. I was so tired of being cold, of being hungry and weak, of fighting to stay alive. I almost fell asleep, but a hope deep in my gut spurred me on. I pulled myself up and kept walking through the woods, down into a gully to a frosty stream, and up the hill on the other side.

When I emerged from the trees, evening had come. Half frozen and weak, I lifted my head to scan the snow-covered meadow. A fence extended into the distance and disappeared behind a gray building that reminded me of the toolshed where I was born. A smaller building lay beyond it. I stood there, staring for a few moments, hardly believing my eyes. I sniffed the air and caught a hint of smoke—like the scent of the man who left us in the prairie. If there was a man around, it could at least be a place to get warm and renew my strength. I was overwhelmed with an odd mix of feelings that I couldn't sort out. Altering my course, I aimed for the barn. The hope of finding a dry place out of the weather gave me renewed energy. My steps quickened as I traipsed through the snow.

By the time the old barn towered over me, my paws were numb. The sky had darkened, and I was wet and shivering. I crept through a hole in one of the weathered boards into a vast, dimly lit world of machinery and pungent smells. With the last of my energy I burrowed down into the nearest pile of straw and fell into a deep peaceful sleep for the first time in days.

I dreamt I walked through an airy green meadow full of spicy-scented flowers and butterflies with a warm breeze sweeping over me. Mice waited everywhere, in the grass and among the flowers—ready to be chased and caught and eaten.

The crow of a rooster awakened me. I poked my head out of my bed of straw to morning light streaming through cracks in the gray wall. I stretched, yawned and breathed in a dozen strong scents all mixed together. When I inspected my surroundings, I found I was not the only animal in the big barn. A huge cow with a sweet warm odor stood in the far corner, shifting her weight. She shook her massive head, clanking the bell that hung around her neck. When I meowed, she looked at me, bellowed, and then turned her head away. The scent of other cats caught my attention, but I didn't see them around.

Plenty of mice lived in the barn, too, and it didn't take long to catch one. As I greedily consumed the first substantial meal I'd eaten in days, I decided to stay awhile.

While I finished the last bite, three white chickens ducked into the barn through the same breach I had entered the night before. They looked comical, strutting around with bobbing heads, clucking and pecking about in the straw. A few more chickens soon followed. Before long the barn floor was alive with the silly birds. I got too close to one. It squawked and pecked me on my head. I hissed at it with arched back and decided to keep my distance.

The noisy chicken chatter obscured the sound of the barn door swinging open. A stream of light spread over the dirt floor. Quickly hiding behind a bale of hay, I waited, tense and ready to run. I peeked around the corner. My heart sank—a man! I'd hoped I wouldn't run into him so soon. Just when I found a place out of the weather with good hunting.

The man, his middle round under his blue clothes, carried a bucket and plodded to the corner of the barn where the cow waited. She turned to watch him and bellowed. The man patted her neck, poured some grain into a bin, and made mellow sounds. He sat on a stool beside the placid beast and collected milk in the bucket. I peeked from my hiding place. Fascinating! I licked my lips, my whiskers and nose quivering. The man groaned as he rose to his feet again, picked up the bucket and left the barn.

I came out of hiding and peered outside. The man walked between two large trees toward a white house at the far end of a large snow-covered area. A birdbath sat askew under one of the trees. Several ears of dried corn hung from a low branch of the other. A small white shed stood alongside the fence.

The man disappeared into the house. I turned to go back in the barn when the bark of a dog startled me. The dog was burly, black, and running toward me. Racing into the barn, I scrambled up a stack of hay bales. His teeth flashed white as he barked and scratched at the bottom of the pile—too close for me. My heart pounded. The bale beneath me shifted. Would it topple? I took a flying leap onto a diagonal timber and up to the loft. When I was out of sight, the dog retreated.

I smelled the other cats and turned around. There were two of them, both females. One hefty with gray stripes, and the other, gold like our mother with big green eyes. They were much older than I and standoffish. I meowed a greeting; the gray one acknowledged my presence with a meow, and the other pulled her chin in and turned her head. They both wandered off to different parts of the big loft, marking their territory as they went. Most unfriendly.

Though there would be dangers living in the barn, I could stay out of the weather and eat all I wanted. It had to be better than life in the prairie grass or the woods I had crossed. The loft afforded a great view of the barn below. I claimed my sleeping spot, far from the nests of the other cats.

The next few days, I explored the rest of the barn, and the pastures and fields surrounding it. I noted the comings and goings of the man and the other animals. The dog never came in the barn at night and not much during the day. He couldn't climb the plank ladder to the loft. I was safe there.

The fat chickens wandered in and out of the barn during the day. At night they returned to the white shed close by and did not return until the next morning.

The other cats didn't seem interested in much but the mice and each other. I never saw them around the man or any of the other animals. I'm not sure the man knew they lived in the barn. I wanted to play and tried to be friendly, but they were not impressed with me and ignored me most of the time.

The man came and went regularly to tend to the cow. Every morning he collected her milk, then she left to spend the day in the pasture. When the man returned from taking the milk to the house every morning, he cleaned out the cow's stall, whistling as he went about his work. He moved so slowly, I could easily outrun him if he ever discovered me. Even so, I always watched him from the safety of the loft. If I remained careful he might never know I was around.

Every evening, the man came back with the cow, her bell clanking with every heavy step. He did the milking thing again. The smell of milk made my mouth water. I wanted so to taste it. One chilly morning the man left a pan of warm milk on the barn floor just outside the cow's stall. I couldn't resist sampling it. I hadn't had milk since we were taken away from our mother. It tasted wonderful! I couldn't stop myself from drinking it all. But I was very careful. I don't think the man knew who stole it.

Then the strangest thing happened. The man began to leave the pan of milk there often on cold mornings and never seemed upset when it was gone. I always waited until he left the barn before coming down from the loft to lap the pan clean. The other cats preferred mice and never came to drink the milk, but I loved it.

The man glanced toward the rafters one morning after putting the pan of milk down, and he saw me looking at him. I shrank back. He didn't make angry noises. Instead, he spoke in gentle sounds, the corners of his eyes crinkling slightly. Did he know all along it was me who drank the milk? He didn't seem to mind. I was careful all the same and waited until he was gone. I couldn't be sure what he might do if I got too close.

During that long winter, I got careless and started to sneak out of the hayloft as soon as he came into the barn to milk the cow. I stayed at a distance as he aimed a stream of milk and splashed it into the pan. I always waited until he turned his back before I approached then cautiously watched him as I drank.

He talked to me every day as he milked, glancing my way only occasionally, and I began to get used to the sound of his voice. Before I knew it, I looked forward to not only the milk, but to his company.

One day as I came to drink from the pan, the man suddenly shouted. I looked up with wide eyes and ran to the safety of the loft. What did I do to make him angry? I looked down, trembling, and saw the bucket had fallen over—the milk soaking into the straw on the floor. The man kicked at the timber just below me. Then he stopped, looked around, and up at me in the loft. I crouched down with tail wrapped around me and ears back. The man made friendly sounds, but I wasn't about to come down again.

And I didn't—not for many days—until the man had left the barn. He continued to leave the milk there at the corner of the cow's stall and always peered up at me and spoke with soft sounds when he saw me looking at him.

Nothing changed for a long time. He talked nice to me every day when he finished milking as I looked down from the loft, hesitant to trust him. The sounds he made were always a mystery to me, but over time I could see he was not like the other men. I began to think that whatever happened when he shouted that day, did not matter now. Before winter was over, I again came down when I saw him coming, and he talked to me while he milked the cow.

Most mornings, after I drank the milk, I meowed a thank you to the man. He always looked at me with soft kind eyes. I could tell he liked me, and it made me feel warm inside.

One early spring day, after I finished his offering, I glanced up at the man while he rubbed the cow's neck. I meowed, pointing my ears forward. He looked down at me. I studied the man's face and his hands as they stroked her, remembering how it felt to be touched. It had been so long since I felt the warmth of another body, so long since I felt connected to someone. The man put out his hand to me, but I backed away, afraid to trust him, though I wanted to.

It took several days before I found the courage to sniff his hand, and several more before I let him touch me. Then one day after he had finished the milking, I walked over with my head and tail held high and rubbed my whole body against his pant leg. He murmured to me gently and reached down. I shrank back momentarily, sniffed at his finger, and then pushed my head into his hand to tell him it was okay. I closed my eyes and purred as he stroked me between my ears and down my back. It felt like home.

Warm weather came and brought with it sweet remembrances of the carefree days with my brothers and sisters. Again, I chased bugs and little green lizards—just for fun—and watched the squirrels in the trees between the barn and the house. Nearly grown by then, I could run fast and continued to hunt mice; they rarely got away. In the afternoons, I frolicked in the pasture that lay beyond the barn, catching the scents of spring flowers. I jumped at butterflies and meowed at the cow, of whom I had become very fond.

I began to follow the man around as he did his chores. Every morning we went to the shed where the chickens spent the night. He collected eggs from their nests. When he milked the cow, I was always there, and when he cleaned out her stall, too. I welcomed the times he reached down to stroke my fur and reminded him by rubbing along his leg if he forgot. By summer, the man and I were true friends.

I have become well acquainted with the other animals on the farm, too. The cats are not as unfriendly as they were, but they often confuse me. They either ignore me or follow me around yowling for my attention. The black dog and I have come to an uneasy truce, and he never barks at me anymore. The chickens have accepted me without concern. Sometimes I chase them a little, but they know it is only a game, and often chase me back. I never go hungry now. The man still gives me a little milk every day, but I rarely eat the mice I catch. Instead, I usually bring them to him. In exchange, the man gives me delicious food from a can with the most wonderful smell.

My life is good now; the man and I are best friends. Don't get me wrong—I'm still suspicious of most people. I never let strangers get close to me. But sometimes on warm days when the man is resting on the porch, I curl up in his lap and take a nap on his soft blue belly. I dream of my mother and my squirming brothers and sisters curled up together on our tattered blanket.

6.
Half-Price Cats
Carol Murphy

I saw in the local newspaper a piece about the SPCA offering to let folks adopt their cats for half the price. Seems like the SPCA had too many cats- well over 200 was the figure. After reading this, I threw my paper across the room. I had just about reached my limit in frustration with so-called cat people.

It all started with my husband who insisted we needed a mouser, a gopher getter, a critter exterminator. We have five acres and he was getting tired of setting traps. Every morning I would see him check the ten traps around the upper acreage. The lower part was just adding too much land to this routine, and anyway, the horses were down there in the pasture munching on grass, hopefully tromping on gophers.

"You mean we need to get a cat", I replied.

"Probably more than one," he sighed loudly and looked up from setting the latest trap. He had a bucket full of traps and estimated that in the last year he had gotten about 100 gophers. At first he was sort of like the angler who goes out fishing and has a really good day. As I drove into the garage coming home from work, he would hurry over to my car. "Today I got three!" he bragged. Not anymore. I could see the desperation in his eyes.

So, low and behold, one day my neighbor who rented the house next door, was sitting outside on the porch smoking, a huge packing box next to her, when I took the Bulldog for a walk. She waved.

"Hi!" I waved back. "What's with the box?"

"We have to move. The owners are coming back. I thought I had another year here, but, well, you know the economy." She blew smoke upwards and sideways. I used to do that when I smoked and I thought I was being cool. Now it just looked gross. "I am just so worried about what I will do with my cats," she added sadly as she looked into the distance and blew another puff of smoke.

Bingo! The answer to my husband's hopelessness was right next door. "What kind of cats?" This almost was too coincidental to be true.

"Just two, plain short-haired cats. One is a sort of a scaredy-cat and the other one is a little stand offish sometimes, but they're great buddies. I have had them since my sons were little, and the place I found to move into does not allow animals." A tear trickled down her cheek.

"Do they hunt? Are they good mousers?" The neighbor had her memories. I had a mission.

"That's why we got them, to hunt mice. The big one caught bats."

"Bats?" I looked up into the trees apprehensively. "I haven't seen one of those. I guess I really do need cats now that you've added bats to the critter list," I said. "Let me see them."

"Really? I have to look for them" She stood up. "With all the moving men, they hid." So she looked inside, outside and all around. No cats.

"They're just frightened. Come back and I will have them for you to meet. The big one is Bill and little one is Toby."

I should have heeded this blatant prediction. Bill is my husband's name. All he said when I told him was, "We'll take them."

Mistake number one: Never tell a moving neighbor you will take their cats, especially if one kitty has your husband's name. Moving neighbors are desperate.

Two days later, the cats were still in hiding, although she assured me they were just worried about all the activity. I agreed to take the cats without seeing them because she was so grateful and I really, truly, honestly did need them.

Mistake number two: Remember mistake number one, especially with cats.

On moving day, her son and husband came over with two cats in crates, a tiny grey one stuck to the back of his crate in fright and a larger white hunkered down inside his crate eyeing me worriedly.

I told the two men, "I'll wait till you're gone, close the garage door, open the crates and leave them in here for a couple of weeks to get them used to us, then move them to the barn for a week before I let them outside. That's what the vet suggested." They shrugged. Guys don't care, and even if they did, they don't usually show it, especially with cats. But, after all, I did have cats before, so I smugly thought I knew what I was doing.

Mistake number three: Cats have their own opinions. Cats do not care what vets say or what experience humans have with other cats.

After two weeks of feeding, watering and cleaning, Bill was getting friendly and actually purring when he saw me, but I had not yet seen Toby. My husband and I looked everywhere in the garage, but you know garages, a virtual haven for cats that like to hide. Our garage could have won a medal. No luck. So, when I moved Bill to the barn which was to be their permanent home, still no little cat. For several days, I could tell Toby was eating and drinking and using his potty box. Bill went into the barn but immediately hid behind horse jumps and wouldn't come out. I finally realized these cats were not outside cats, not very friendly, and probably I had been had. Even when I called, "Bill, Bill", which was very weird to begin with, he never came to me again, although my husband yelled, "What? What?" several times.

I left the barn door open.

The renter from next door who had given me the cats moved away and the owners of the house moved back. A month later, the couple waved at me from their porch when they saw me walking the Bulldog. "Hey", said the man, "I think I saw Bill sitting by our glass door on the patio. He looked very confused."

Beyond doubt, if that cat came back, I would immediately change his name.

"Well, at least I know he is okay." I replied.

He continued. "I tried shoving him through the fence, but he came running back. What do you want to do? He's eating with our cats and going in and out of the garage."

"If he's okay, just feed him. Apparently he didn't like us." Thank God he did not ask me about the other one. Maybe he felt sorry for Bill. He and his wife already had three cats of their own. Maybe this was how people started cat collections. Neighborhood cats just kept arriving.

But on to the next thought – feral cats. It seemed like a good idea. After all, they needed homes, liked to hunt, and liked barns. The bottom line was the sort of cat that worked for dinner. We have a local rescue group that saves these felines, neuters or spays them, gives them their shots, and then places them.

Mistake number four: Never work with people who have dedicated their lives to wild cats.

"Well, how about feral cats?" I suggested to my husband who was still setting traps.

"What are those?" he asked.

"Wild cats."

"Do they bite?' he asked, finally looking up from his golf magazine, intrigued.

"Well, you remember Satieva?" I reminded him. Our son had trapped a young cat in the forests of Carmel Valley and had raised him. Satieva bit sometimes, but he was an awesome critter removal specialist. But the problem was his name, Satieva, you know like Satieva Cannibus. For those of you who don't know a lot of Latin, that's marijuana. I would yell outside and around the neighborhood, "SATIEVA!"

Finally a neighbor asked, "Do you know what that means?"

"No," was all I answered.

"Well, look it up," was all he said.

I never liked that particular neighbor.

My son has an interesting sense of humor. But Satieva was the kind of cat we needed now.

"What about the Bulldog?" My husband reached down to rub her ears. "Will they bother her?"

"She's an old person's dog. She just lays around inside the house."

I called the feral cat project folks. The woman who called back had a very nice deceiving phone demeanor. She intensely interviewed me about my house, what the barn was made of, and told me about the feral cats they had that were being spayed or neutered and would be up for adoption after the yearly fund raiser. She wanted to see my place. I was gratefully hopeful, and a little impressed, and told her when I would be home. We made a date.

Of course, why would I not guess that she would make a surprise visit on a day when Bill (my husband) was painting the deck and I was at work? I guess getting feral cats is almost like adopting babies. I think social workers make surprise visits too.

As soon as I got home, my husband met me in the garage and bellowed, "Those feral cat people are weird!" My husband likes to speak loudly to make a point.

Oh, boy. This was not looking good. "Did she come today?" I asked.

"Did she come? As soon as she got out of the car, she said 'your place is too sterile'. What do you think of that? All day I work to make this place look good and she said it's too sterile! She didn't even look behind the house and told me she was expecting a wooden barn."

"She must have had some picture in her mind of a dilapidated falling down wooden structure with crates all over. That's silly. I told her we had a prefabricated barn with 5 stalls." My horses liked the barn. Even the Bulldog did, when she made the decision to go outside. Bulldogs make their own choices, but that is another story.

I decided to go to the local SPCA to find a cat. I called my friend who is almost a vet but without the degree and she said she'd go along to help me pick out a cat.

Mistake number five: Always learn the proper wording to use with animal shelter volunteers. Apparently they have power.

On the way, my friend attempted to educate me on the proper verbiage. "Now, if they ask you if you want a male or female, never say you don't care. Say you have no preference. And, if they ask you where the cat is going to live, do not say in a barn. Say in a spare bedroom with its own bed, with lots of fluffy pillows."

"This is stupid. The cats are going to be indoor-outdoor cats. I can't lie."

"I am telling you, lie", she said looking out the window, clearly disgusted.

When we arrived, there were lots of would-be adopters standing around with several volunteers. There was a volunteer supervising the other volunteers, who also was a sort of general information giver, there was a volunteer for the dogs, a volunteer for the larger animals, a volunteer for the birds, and, of course, a volunteer for the cats.

The cat volunteer showed us into the small room with all of the cats in wire cages. Some of them had signs that said Not Adoptable which made no sense since they were housed in a room with a sign that read "Cats for Adoption". Then, unfortunately for me, I told the truth.

"What kind of cat are you looking for?" she asked all smiles.

"Well, I don't care if it's a boy or girl, but I hope it can catch mice because we have a barn full."

My friend walked away.

The cat volunteer lady looked at me, hard, and quit smiling. Immediately I knew my friend had been right. "Our cats need loving homes, not barns. Cats need to be inside, away from predators."

I thought a cat was a predator. That's why I wanted one.

"Where did you find this one?" I asked pointing to a cat that had stray printed on the description card pasted to the front of its cage.

"Well, he was found on a local rural road." Her hand lingered lovingly on the cage as if she was visualizing this poor creature wandering all alone on a busy highway.

"Look". I interrupted her reverie. "A road is outdoors. That is what I want, an outside cat."

Her beady eyes stared through me. "Maybe I could give you the name of the feral cat organization."

I sighed. "No, I tried them. They said our barn was too sterile." It was about this time that a second SPCA volunteer came into the room with another customer, and she overheard my comment.

"Did you say that you already called them? Well, what happened? We are here to help people, so if something did not go well, we should be informed." And she smiled brightly as if she were on my side.

But now I was finally wising up.

"Look, I don't really want to get into a discussion about another organization. I just want a cat." I was almost begging and I had learned my lesson- lie. I gave up. Maybe there was a cat or two out there for me, but apparently none of these people were going to help me find one. What a sad state of affairs when a good solid citizen cannot adopt a cat to run and frolic in a huge barn with lots of room to hunt and play.

But this story does have a happy ending. I did finally adopt two wonderful cats from a shelter far, far away, one that I won't name because, well, you can figure that out for yourself. I think their adoption was meant to be because the volunteers at the far away shelter said they had put the cats together one night and they ended up being great friends. The volunteers always hoped they would both go to the same home. Maybe this was why everything happened. They love the barn, the house, and even the Bulldog. One hits at her when she walks by and always just misses, but I think he intends to miss. We call them Smokey and the Bandit.

I wrote this story to provide counseling to the well-intentioned, hopeful cat adopters. Run from neighbors who have cats they have to get rid of before they move, do not trust people who have charged themselves with overseeing wild cats, and learn the correct cat terms before you speak with a feline volunteer. But, maybe in the end, some day, after really looking, you will get that special cat.

7.
Hamilton and Bianca
William Doreski

Hamilton and Bianca, siblings,
look fresh as bread from the bakery.
White-dominant calico
Bianca, reddish-splotched white guy
Hamilton arrive attached

as if still in the womb.   Spaying
almost undoes Bianca.   Careless,
sloppy work allotted shelter cats
leaves her so loosely half-stitched
she almost spills her innards

and has to see a second vet
for repair.   Separated, caged,
the siblings droop like daffodils.
Hamilton tries to befriend
his neighbor, but pines for his sister.

She curls into a seashell-shape
and refuses, when petted, to purr.
The life of the big room grinds on.
Bianca heals, but she's sorry
she ever became a cat.   A couple

employed by MIT arrive,
embrace the siblings, depart
with two cat carriers brimming.
A week later a chronicle,
with photos: brother and sister

playing, eating, trailing after
their doting human companions.
The last photo: two cats curled
together so tightly they merge.
The caption: "All tuckered out."

8.
Hanging onto The Coattails of Time
Winston Plowes

For Squeak

The songbirds gone, the dawn hangs dead
The milk's turned brown within your bowl
You cried to get onto the bed

Fighting shadows in your head
You're slow to wake and take control
The songbirds gone, the dawn hangs dead

Your knotted stomach can't be fed
Your fur's a tent with ribs as poles
You cried to get onto the bed

The day's approaching we both dread
Where pieces no more make the whole
The songbirds gone, the dawn hangs dead

You lived far longer than they said
And leave behind a love shaped hole
You cried to get onto the bed

The opal eyes that fill your head
Don't see the nine lives darkness stole
The songbirds gone, the dawn hangs dead
You cried to get onto the bed

Winston Plowes lives aboard his floating home with his cat, *Fatty* in the north of England. In the past year he has collaborated with *The Arvon Foundation, the BBC, Glastonbury Festival, UCLAN* and *Manchester Museum*. He regularly tutors for *The Square Chapel*, Halifax and in schools. Winston was *Poet in Residence* for the *Rochdale Canal Festival* in 2012 and *The Hebden Bridge Arts Festival* 2012-14. Jointly self-published in *Misery Begins at Home*, 2010 and micro Chapbook *Extras*, 2014. His first solo collection of surrealist poetry *Telephones, Love Hearts & Jellyfish, Electric Press* is out this fall. Winston is also inventor of the world's first (and possibly last) *Random Poetry Generating Bicycle, The Spoke-n-Word*.

www.winstonplowes.co.uk

9.
Lions... The Biggest Cats
Mark Hudson

I was walking in Chicago with my friend Barbara
when we walked by a restaurant.   She said, "I'll never
eat in that restaurant again.   They kill endangered species."
She then told me of a news story where there was a
controversy about a man who was killing lions in Africa,
endangered species.

The next day, I was on the train and I came across
a section of the New York Times.   I picked it up and
read it.   There was the story of the safari hunter who
paid like a million dollars to hunt lions, an endangered
species.   I guess the ethical question it brings up is,
could the money be better well spent?

Then I read the rest of the articles on the page,
and I read about bloodshed in the Middle East,
wars and rumors of wars, and humans killing humans
on almost every square inch of this planet.   It brings
up another question of ethics, does it make sense
to be concerned about the death of animals when
human beings are dying just as quickly?

I was at the Library, and I happened to
open up a National Geographic to a photo of
a man in Africa who got his arms bitten off by a lion.
It was an image that haunts me to this day.
Of course, the lion was probably just defending
him or herself, or their breed.   It brings up
the question of whether eating meat is ethical,
and we'd be better off eating vegetables.

In the Bible, it says one day the lion
will lay down with the lamb. If I interpret that
correctly, one day there will be peace restored
to the people of Earth, and perhaps even the
animals as well. Not to sound too Biblical,
but I find it interesting that God created
animals before man, and on Noah's Ark,
he saved two of the species, but only
Noah and family. A while back, I was
in church and heard Bill Cosby's narration
of Noah's Ark. He who laughs first, laughs last.

Where are you from?
Evanston, Illinois.

Describe in one or two sentences how being friends with a cat has enriched your life.
I had a girlfriend once who had three cats.   She said, "If you won't love my cats, you can't love me." So I learned to love the cats.

Do you have any other pets; if so, what are their breeds and names?
I have a Guinea pig named Willow. I've had him for five years, he's awesome.

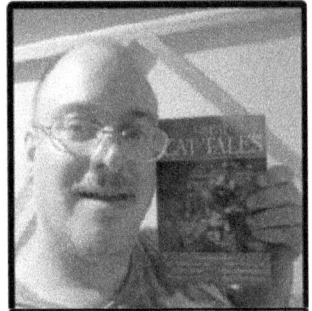

If you are a writer (either by trade or compulsion) what first drew you to the craft? If you're not a writer, why did you choose to write a piece for this anthology?
I've been writing and drawing since I was little. I hope to keep it going as long as possible.

10.
Living with Man's Other Friend
Arthur Carey

Tigger II sits outside the patio door, fixing me with an accusing stare, one of her attempts at mind control. The winter day is cold and rainy. Birds are few, and the squirrels transit the top of the backyard fence rather than play "catch me if you can" on the wet ground.

We are engaged, Tigger and I, in a continuing battle of wills to determine who will be inconvenienced first by the other. I command the portal of ingress and egress, the glass door separating comfort and sustenance from adventure and cold. Shall I interrupt my reading to rise and open the door? Her immediate goal is gaining entrance. After that, she will inspect the food dish yet again and assert ownership of the sofa by the living room window. We understand our roles. Eventually, we both know, I shall admit her. But on whose terms?

Tigger II, so called because my wife and I have a friend with a pet of the same name, was captured (or kittennapped) hissing and scratching from hiding in bushes with other feral family members. She is a rescue cat, saved from a brief and uncertain life by volunteers who donate their time, energy, and care to saving the lives of cats. Lucky cat.

Does she appreciate the generosity of patrons who have saved her from starvation, illness, or worse? Of course not. She is a cat. The ancient Egyptians didn't worship dogs, man's best friend. They understood dogs. Cats are more complex and less open in their dealings with humans.

When we had dogs, Skippy and Brandy, they would reward us unfailingly with boundless gratitude, offering wet tongues and squirming appreciation for simple recognition. But cats view their mere existence as a gift in itself. If a stranger comes to the front door, a dog races about in warning mode, signaling the arrival in a frenzy of barking. *Danger! Intruder! But I'm on guard!* But our cats, however, react with a more calculated, me-first response—absence. *Whoa! What's that...? I'd better find a hidey-hole until the two-legs sort things out and restore tranquility to my world.*

Meanwhile, Tigger waits impatiently on the doorstep, still engaging me with accusing eyes. Occasionally, she will open her mouth and meow. That several inches of double pane glass between us separate sound and audience matters little. It is the gesture, the "hurry along, I'm being inconvenienced again" message. Usually it works. I am motivated to respond the way adult birds at a nest respond to the demanding, open mouths of their young.

This is our fifth cat. Tigger is almost six in human years, a middle-aged forty or so for a cat. My wife and I have outlived, if not outwitted, her four predecessors. First came Samantha, a brown and gray tabby that joined us in the 1960s, named for the star of a popular television show about a witch. Samantha roamed our tri-level home in Grand Rapids, Michigan, shortly after we were married. As a kitten, she survived with aplomb falling from a second floor landing to the first floor. She enjoyed crouching, Snoopy-like, atop the kitchen cabinets, smugly peering down at us. *See what I can do, you two-legs anchored to the floor?* She greeted guests with enthusiasm, often when they least expected it. My wife and I awoke to a scream one night. It was my visiting mother, sleeping on a sofa bed in the basement. Samantha had decided my mother would make a soft landing spot for her leap from the top of the bed.

Chere came next, another brown and gray tabby. She followed us by air to Stockton, California, in 1967. We impressed friends with our love of animals, our deep pockets, or our poor judgment. Once children arrived, Chere accepted the loss of attention grudgingly. And on the night before we embarked for Los Angeles where I was to enroll in graduate school at UCLA, Chere vanished after the arrival of the movers. She had suffered enough people-induced upheaval in her life. Cats are sensitive.

In the 1970s, our son Brian, seven, and daughter Lisa, six, decided they wanted a cat. So young...so trusting...so adept at bending parents to their wishes—just like a cat. We scheduled another trip to an animal shelter. The children selected a tiny, feisty, black and white kitten and promptly dubbed it "Rocky" after Sylvester Stallone in the film of the same name. Rocky was female but gender was overlooked at the sight of her batting pieces of crumpled paper dangled from string. Then, one Mother's Day, the children gave my wife a present in a hastily wrapped shoebox. Something inside made scratching noises. Surprise! An orange and white male kitten poked its head out and joined the family. The kitten had six toes on one foot so it promptly became known as Big Foot. Rocky and Big Foot co-existed, amicably for the most part, living to the ripe old ages of nineteen and eighteen in human years.

So now we have Tigger. (Or she has us.) Her wild origin manifests itself occasionally in a careful bite when she is offended. It is a toothy shot across the bow that never breaks skin, a carefully calculated warning to desist from picking her up when she is in cranky mode, which is often.

But cats are cautious, ever mindful of the importance of links in the food chain from refrigerator to dish. Tigger has a dinner bell that rings about four o'clock when she sees me at the kitchen window. She hurries to the patio door awaiting dinner. A thoughtful provider herself, Tigger brings an occasional bird, often living, to the door. Mice she disdains—or can't catch. *See what I did? Can you catch a bird? Silly question.* Because she has a soft mouth and isn't hungry, I rescue and release most of her unlucky catches. I suspended our bird feeders high above the ground. I have seen Tigger leap more than five and a half feet from a sitting position. Is there an Olympics for cats?

Of all our cats, she is the most demanding of human attention. When they are in the mood, cats often suck up to their human providers by feigning affection. Big Foot liked to prowl the back of a sofa to where I was sitting while watching TV and doze with his head on my shoulder. Tigger is insistent about evening naptime, snoozing in a sprawl across our legs as my wife and I sit reading. This is a compromise. She has been banished from our bed due to a propensity to awaken at first light and to bound across my chest to the window to see what has transpired in the backyard overnight.

As my wife and I age, we tend to talk to each other less. What is there to say that has not been said after fifty years of marriage? Ah, but Tigger provides fresh grist for conversation. *Is the cat in or out? When did you see the cat last? Does she have food? Why is she scratching so much? Off! Get off my chair!*

Clawed despoiler of furniture... shedder of hair... pursuer of birds... mother lode of veterinarians... she is all of these. But when Tigger curls up on my legs, closes her eyes, and purrs herself to sleep, she rules again as mistress of the manor. And we wouldn't have it any other way.

11.
Love Is Blind
Mark Hudson

There was a woman in my building who is
almost entirely blind. She had a cat as her companion,
which I'm sure brought her great comfort, living alone.

One day, I think the maintenance man who
had been there just about forever left the company,
but nobody really told me. But I heard him talking
about it, and I haven't seen him since.

One day, I'm walking by the office, and I
guess the new maintenance man, apparently, seems
to be discussing with the landlady something to
do with going into the lady's apartment and
smelling foul stenches that he was unable to handle.

I'm immediately stereotyping the guy as
a jerk. How can you pick on a blind lady, and
her cat, her only companion in the world?

I'm telling my friend Chris about this,
because he was talking about cats. He says,
"Well, you can't take on the problems of
the world. You might not know what the exact
situation is. Don't worry about it."

So, last night, I saw the lady who is
partially blind outside of my apartment.
Curious to find out what happened, I say,
"How is your cat doing?"

She says, "I had a cat for twenty-two
years, but it died three weeks ago. I wasn't
going to get a new one, but my veterinarian
called me and she happened to have a new
one that needed a home. So she happened
to call me, and I got the cat for free. I'm
happy to have another cat, but it will take
a while to get used to my new one."

So my friend Chris was right.
As my dad always used to say, stay out
of office politics. And yes, sometimes
even beautiful animals stink, just like
we humans do as well. But it's just
like the one-time hit song by the
J. Geils Band, "Love Stinks!" and
when a pet passes away, it stinks in general.

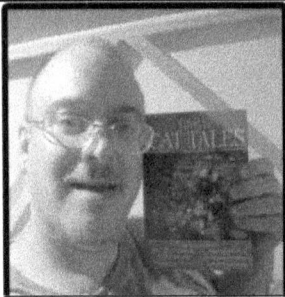

Where are you from?
Evanston, Illinois.

Describe in one or two sentences how being friends with a cat has enriched your life.
I had a girlfriend once who had three cats.   She said, "If you won't love my cats, you can't love me." So I learned to love the cats.

Do you have any other pets; if so, what are their breeds and names?
I have a Guinea pig named Willow.   I've had him for five years, he's awesome.

If you are a writer (either by trade or compulsion) what first drew you to the craft? If you're not a writer, why did you choose to write a piece for this anthology?
I've been writing and drawing since I was little.   I hope to keep it going as long as possible.

12.
Mistaken Identity
Beth Lynn Clegg

I'd noticed the man shortly after moving to the apartment complex. My initial reaction hadn't changed. He gave me the creeps. From his brownish-gray hair to his brown loafer-shod feet he appeared to be a monochromatic array of worn cloth and wrinkled skin on a slender frame. I suppressed a laugh as the image of a plump, but faded, Tootsie Roll flashed across my mind. But, this was no laughing matter. He was back, I was nervous, and he was walking toward me.

It was like that Erin Brocovich movie with Julia Roberts when she was sitting at a bar waiting for a cup of coffee and this guy gives her the eye and she switched her coffee order to go. This guy created that same unease, but there wasn't a Starbucks in sight.

I'd thought it would be safe here. How had he gotten in? Well, that was a no-brainer. The gates are open during office hours giving easy access to any and all comers. Okay. What to do? I couldn't high-tail it inside my unit and leave Tex out. Cats are supposed to be supervised. I called out in hopes he'd come running, which was what I longed to do. A deep voice interrupted my mental gymnastics.

"So, that's Tex? He your cat?" He was standing less than three feet from me, smiling. My voice was shaky when I responded. Shaky? How ridiculous. Why was I frightened? It was midday. We were standing on interconnecting sidewalks in a large open area within shouting distance of swimming pool full of residents.

Beyond that, there was something about him. Something contradictory to his drab countenance. It was his eyes. They literally sparkled with kindness when he said, "My apartment's back yonder, over close to the bayou. Got at least twenty or thirty cats. Feed 'em every morning and evening. People move out and just leave 'em to fend for themselves. I'll never understand it. Four of 'em stay on my porch so I've claimed 'em as mine, but the rest just show up at feedin' time. Every one's got a name. There's Bonnie and Clyde, Sonny and Cher, Dizzy Dean, Shirley and Louise, Frank Sinatra, John F. Kennedy, Ronald Regan, Johnny Cash, Reba, well, you get the idea. When Sammy Davis, Jr., a sweet young kitten, took sickly, I took him to the vet. Guess you could say even though I love 'em I don't know a lot about cats. He went to the vet Sammy Davis, Jr. and came home Oprah Winfrey."

Beth Lynn Clegg, Houston, Texas is an octogenarian who has been published in a variety of genre since beginning her writing career after pursuing other endeavors. An animal lover with two cats, she also enjoys time spent with family and friends, reading, gardening, cooking, and church activities.

13.
Morton Grove Milo
Mark Hudson

A photo came from Morton Grove Animal Shelter,
of a cat named Milo who had been burned.
They gave Milo priority, all the helpers.
They put him ahead of all their concerns.
Forty percent of the gray and white skin,
of this cat was burned and destroyed.
They thought boiling water was poured on him,
he was shipped to Arkansas, his death to avoid.
Milo had surgery, his damaged skin removed,
they say it will take up to four months to recover.
But the story to me was what totally proved,
what can be done to help cats by animal lovers.

Where are you from?
Evanston, Illinois.

Describe in one or two sentences how being friends with a cat has enriched your life.
I had a girlfriend once who had three cats.   She said, "If you won't love my cats, you can't love me." So I learned to love the cats.

Do you have any other pets; if so, what are their breeds and names?
I have a Guinea pig named Willow.   I've had him for five years, he's awesome.

If you are a writer (either by trade or compulsion) what first drew you to the craft? If you're not a writer, why did you choose to write a piece for this anthology?
I've been writing and drawing since I was little.   I hope to keep it going as long as possible.

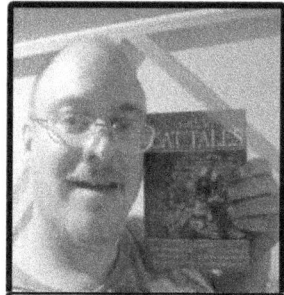

14.
New Kitten
C. Flynt

There's a new kitten at the Johnson house.

Last year's kitten does not approve. One cat is all the cats the Johnsons need. But the scent of the new-born brought out maternal instincts, and if Bringer-Of-Food and Tummy-Scritcher wanted a new kitten, she would oblige.

New-Kitten was fretting, so the old kitten curled up on the blanket next to it and purred until it stopped fretting and went to sleep.

"Aren't they cute? I told you Punkin would like the new baby."

"Are you sure she's safe? What if the cat scratches her?"

"If she gets scratched, we'll hear about it even without the baby monitor. Don't worry."

New-Kitten turned out to be more useful than Punkin expected. It leaked milk whenever it ate and then needed to be washed. It would nestle its head deep into Punkin's fur and its breath was warm. It almost learned to purr.

But New-Kitten was not very smart. Months later, when it should have been frolicking and playing, it was still just gurgling and eating.

Punkin would help it roll onto its tummy and show it how to stand up, but more months passed before the new kitten finally learned to support itself.   Punkin had to nudge her hindquarters before she took her first step.

"Bad, Punkin.   Don't push baby over when she's learning to crawl!"

Punkin was pulled aside and banished from the nursery. Later that night she snuck back in to continue training New-Kitten and finally to fall asleep cuddling it.

A year later, Punkin was ready to give up on New-Kitten and the entire family.   New-Kitten had finally learned to walk on all fours and might be able to learn to play, but Bringer-Of-Food started making it walk on its hind legs.   Couldn't they see how New-Kitten kept falling over?

Then, one day, almost overnight, New-Kitten learned to walk on its hind legs and Tummy-Scritcher gave it a piece of ribbon to drag around the room.

This was fun! New-Kitten had learned a game they could play together.   They played pull-and-chase until they were so tired they fell asleep curled around each other on the rug by the fireplace.

New-Kitten grew bigger and faster.   But even after she learned to walk without falling she couldn't learn to catch mice. She didn't even hear the mice skittering behind the walls and didn't understand when Punkin would stare, pointing out the mouse with her whiskers.

"What does Punkin see that I don't?"

"Maybe ghosts? She's certainly staring at the wall, isn't she?"

Then New-Kitten was allowed outdoors, and Punkin couldn't follow her. She'd leave early in the morning, while the birds were first chirping by the feeder and Punkin's tail was twitching. She didn't come home until the sun was low in the afternoon sky and the squirrels were running across the yard.

Although New-Kitten never understood hunting mice, she understood catching birds. Some days she brought home a feather to tie onto a string.

"Watch Punkin jump! She really likes the feather!"

"Don't play too rough, Kit. Punkin's not a spring kitten anymore."

As the years passed, New-Kitten got as tall as Bringer-Of-Food, and Punkin lost interest in the feathers and string. It was a lot of effort to catch a feather that wasn't a real bird.

But New-Kitten spent an hour each night sitting at the kitchen table while Punkin slept on her lap. When the moon rose, the two of them went to bed and Punkin curled up next to New-Kitten and purred them both to sleep.

One morning New-Kitten left and didn't return that night. Or the next night. Or the next.

Punkin did everything she could to help her find her way home.

"That damn cat wet on Kit's bed again. What are we going to do?"

"She misses her pet human. Punkin's trying to help her find her way back."

"I wish she'd miss the pillow. Thanksgiving is coming up and I don't want Kit's bed smelling like a litter box."

New-Kitten finally found her way home. She scooped Punkin carefully into her arms and Punkin settled in to purr. New-Kitten smelled different than she remembered, but nothing smelled like she remembered these days.

"Punkin's getting scrawny."

"Well, she's pushing twenty. That's old for a cat. You give her the arthritis pill tonight. She likes it when you feed her."

Then New-Kitten was gone again. It was months later when she returned.

"Hey, Mom, where's Punkin?"

"Honey, I'm sorry. Yesterday. She didn't come for her morning treat. I found her curled up on your pillow. She... she... couldn't move. We rushed her to the vet. They said it was kindest to say goodbye."

"But, but... I never said goodbye to—to—her."

****

Cats are tiny time bombs. Purring and ticking as they tunnel next to your heart, until finally, they explode, leaving shards of memories and a cat-shaped void that nothing can ever completely fill.

But the hole can be patched. There's a new kitten at the Johnson house.

15.
On Finding Four Feral Kittens
Abandoned Beneath Hosta Leaves in Our Side Yard
Carolyn Martin

Five weeks old, we estimate
from their sharp teeth and body weight
and how they slurped our chicken soup
before we knew what or how to feed.

Novices in all things animal,
we could not conceive a mother
who would leave her kids behind. It
only took
an hour before they tugged our urge

to swaddle them in polar fleece
and hold them tight against coyotes
and neglect. But allergies and fear
of broken hearts scratched our itch to
claim

them for our own. We commit, therefore,
to settle them in perfect homes
and vow to remain vigilant
during intensive background checks.

Carolyn Martin is blissfully retired in Clackamas, Oregon, where she gardens, writes and plays with creative friends. Since the only poem she wrote in high school was red-penciled "extremely maudlin," she is still amazed she continues to write. Her poems have appeared in publications such as *Stirring*, *Persimmon Tree*, *Antiphon*, and *Naugatuck River Review*. Her second collection, *The Way a Woman Knows*, was released in February 2015 by The Poetry Box, Portland, OR.

16.
Patriots Room
William Doreski

Kobe, a big fluffy ginger guy,
is boldly round and aggressive.
When I arrive to clean the room

he leans from a cage-top and hugs
and drapes himself around my neck.
He clings there as I vacuum and mop

the floor, clings as I gather the dishes,
then drops back onto the cage
when I set out fresh canned food.

Angelo and Gloria, his friends,
defer to his cuddly bulk.   The room,
the Patriots Room, small and square,

houses a dozen grown cats, each
clawing to maintain a foothold.
Some hunker in cages because

still timid or unsocialized.
Some cluster at the dry food dishes
and swap gossip, rumors, anecdotes.

Most move up and down the furniture,
taking turns at the window,
but Tippy, slick-black and declawed,

can't climb the cages so stays
close to the floor.   Kobe peers down
from his aerie and sneers.   Half

the volunteers fear his big paws,
which they claim he wields too freely.
I don't mind a few scratches, though.

The weight of him around my neck
warms me to the soles of my shoes;
and the way he snugs up to Gloria

and Angelo proves that causes
are never lost, that no cat
is too big and thuggish to love.

17.
Pharaoh
Mark Hudson

Sometimes I choose to walk down alleys. I
suppose I'm supposed to consider myself a functional
person in society, but I know too many people in
this town, and after a while, I don't want to run
into anybody.

So recently, I'm walking down the alley,
and I spot two perfectly good frames that have a
sign that says they are free.

I grab them and walk towards home, and
I see a woman coming out of an apartment,
a partially blind lady from my apartment who
has a cat. She is dropping her cat off at the vet,
in a different apartment building. I believe
she has a friend there who takes her cat to
the vet.

I approach her. "Hi! Dropping your
cat off at the vet?" (I can tell, because she
has an empty cage in her hand.)

"Yes!" she says.

"What's your cat's name?" I ask.

"Pharaoh!" she replies.

"Feral?" I misinterpret.

Then, as I found out, feral means a cat
who is undomesticated.   Like an alley cat.

So it's no surprise that this happened in an alley!

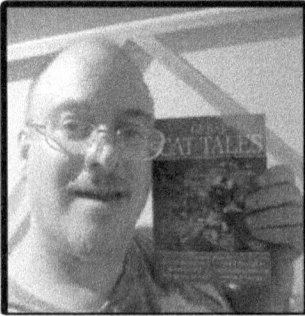

Where are you from?
Evanston, Illinois.

Describe in one or two sentences how being friends with a cat has enriched your life.
I had a girlfriend once who had three cats.   She said, "If you won't love my cats, you can't love me." So I learned to love the cats.

Do you have any other pets; if so, what are their breeds and names?
I have a Guinea pig named Willow.   I've had him for five years, he's awesome.

If you are a writer (either by trade or compulsion) what first drew you to the craft? If you're not a writer, why did you choose to write a piece for this anthology?
I've been writing and drawing since I was little.   I hope to keep it going as long as possible.

18.
Spotty's Story
Anne Wilson

Spotty was a beautiful Siamese cat, named, in case you wondered, by my eleven-year-old son. She was chosen as a cat who would be happy to be an indoors cat because the feral cats in our area of Mallorca suffered from cat flu, a feline form of A.I.D.S. She was affectionate, verbal, and a much loved addition to our lives.

Her name was an unfortunate choice for our Spanish friends, none of whom could pronounce the 's' sound at the beginning of a word. Already baffled by people who would keep a cat inside their home, they called her Es-potty; apart from one school-friend of my sons, Juana-Marie, who used to enter our apartment and shout 'CAT' at the top of her voice whilst looking under all the furniture.

Having previously scoffed at the very idea, I bought a cat-lead and took Spotty for short walks. These were usually as far as the local tapas bar where Spotty liked to climb a tree above the outdoor tables and lie on the low roof tiles until I had finished my café con leche.

On one occasion my son and I went inside and came out to find a group of local men had commandeered a ladder from somewhere and were noisily organising a rescue operation for the 'trapped' cat. Spotty ignored their efforts, descended the tree in the stately manner typical of her breed and joined us for the walk home.

On another occasion, a well-meaning Spanish boyfriend loaded her into his car alongside our picnic things, assuming that cats (perhaps like dogs) accompanied their families on such excursions. My son was delighted. I imagined she would have to remain in the car but Spotty had other ideas. She climbed out and explored no further than a few yards from our picnic blanket the whole afternoon. The day became remembered in family history as 'Spotty's Big Day Out'.

Circumstances were to dictate a reluctant return to England, the worst aspect of this being that the old quarantine laws were still in force; they were changed the year following our departure. Spotty would be condemned to six months in a kennels. This was unthinkable and I made the heart-breaking decision to find her a new home, so she at least could remain on the island.

Boxes were packed. Our apartment was advertised for sale. A buyer was found. Arrangements were pencilled in then confirmed. Completion dates were agreed. Couriers were booked. Flights were booked. Arrangements for temporary accommodation in England were put in place.

All the time I was desperately seeking a new family for Spotty. People either, already had a pet, didn't want a pet, or would have loved to offer her a home but lived on the island only periodically.

Finally, my son and I ended up with a one week time lapse between vacating our apartment and boarding our flight to the UK. Our belongings had gone before us and we were booked into a hotel, the Rosa Del Mar in Magaluf, for our remaining few days. We had two suitcases and a poor trusting cat.

Close to tears, I explained our situation to the hotel receptionist and incredibly he said Spotty could stay in our room with us. As it happened we had a large family room with a balcony. I went over the road to an Aldi store and bought cat litter and a washing up bowl; they had no litter trays.

The following morning, I visited the travel agents to collect our tickets.

Caroline, the woman at the desk was English and as we chatted I broke down in tears of desperation, admitting that in spite of all my efforts I had failed to find a home for our beloved pet. All I did have was the telephone number of a Dutch vet. Caroline told me her husband was Mallorcan and they lived on a small farm in the beautiful area of Valldemosa. She was an animal lover and would take Spotty home that evening.

When the office closed, Spotty, with her basket, and her food dishes and washing up bowl were carefully placed on the back seat of our saviour's car. My heart was breaking, but I cried this time with relief.

Over the next few days I asked myself constantly; *was this really a family of animal lovers or were they just sorry for us? Would Spotty be loved and cared for?*

At the end of the week, on our last day on the island, I unexpectedly had my answer.

Seated on a bus, I was traveling through the city of Palma when my mobile rang. It was Caroline.

Spotty had settled in on the farm. She had made friends with the donkey which she went out and sat beside in the daytime. Occasionally she chased butterflies which, I suppose, she had never seen before. Nor for that matter, had she seen a donkey. But why, oh, why had we christened a Siamese cat 'Spotty'? Caroline's Spanish husband was struggling with the name, which made everyone laugh.

So, I knew her new family didn't plan to change our cat's awkward name, but what really gave me the peace of mind I needed was the actual purpose of Caroline's call; she had forgotten to ask when Spotty's birthday was.

That was the moment I knew I had accidentally encountered just the right family for Spotty.

19.
Steve's Miracle
Amanda Madru

In both appearance and manner, Steve is a strikingly unusual orange tabby. He has double paws on all four feet, his shade of orange is so pale as to closely resemble that of a Creamsicle, and his features are notably sphinx-like. He is singularly attached to his "mother," my sister Lindsay, who adopted him when he was a five month old kitten. When Lindsay goes to work, Steve waits for her at the top of the stairs. When Lindsay ventures outside, Steve watches her from the window in the upstairs hallway. When Lindsay eats dinner, Steve perches atop her shoulder, and when Lindsay sleeps, Steve is curled up beside her. Lindsay, in turn, loves Steve with all her heart. Their bond is extraordinary and unbreakable.

One icy day in mid-January of last year, though, Steve became suddenly and mysteriously ill. That morning, he seemed unable to use that cat box, and Lindsay thought he might be constipated. Reluctantly, she went to work. Shortly after, I got out of bed, Steve vomited. Unaware of the incident with the cat box, I didn't think much of it. I cleaned up the mess and went about my day, but after a few hours, I couldn't help but notice that Steve had not budged from the wicker couch on our sun porch, so I went out to check on him. He barely moved. I began to pet him. "Steve? Are you okay, buddy?"

He barely lifted his head, but when my hand approached his back end, became agitated and hissed at me. I found this reaction unnerving, but I left him alone. When my mother came in, I let her know that I thought something was wrong with Steve, and she then told me that he had been unable to relieve himself that morning. I had a very bad feeling; I wanted to call the vet, but she thought it would be best to wait for Lindsay, and we argued about what to do.

Finally, Lindsay got home, and we informed her that her cat—her baby—was not well. She took him down to the cat box one last time, just to see what he would do. He got into the box, where he crouched and strained, but nothing happened. Something was terribly wrong. "He needs to go to the vet," she stated. There was no longer anything to debate.

It was a Saturday night, and our regular vet was closed, so she called the animal emergency room. They immediately suspected a urinary blockage, a true emergency. My mother and a panicking Lindsay packed Steve into a carrier and rushed off to the veterinary hospital, which is over an hour away. After they left, I sat down to watch football, but for the life of me, I could not focus on the game.

****

As hours passed, the sick feeling in the pit of my stomach grew steadily worse. I tried to call my mother's cell phone, but there was no answer, and I knew it couldn't be good. When the phone rang at long last, I picked it up on the first ring. They were still at the emergency room, it was definitely a urinary blockage, but at that point, they knew nothing more than that. Lindsay, my mother said, was in the hospital's bathroom, throwing up. "I have to go," my mother whispered. "The vet is here." I hung up, but I didn't put the phone back in its cradle. I too wanted to vomit.

Midnight was fast approaching, and I wanted to wait up for my mother and sister, but my eyelids were growing heavier by the minute. I climbed into bed and took out my journal.

Lindsay is hysterical, I wrote. *My heart breaks for her. I hope and pray that Steve will be okay, not only for his own sake, but because I don't think Lindsay will be able to cope with any other outcome... Dear God, if you are there, please, please let Steve be all right, or else somehow give Lindsay the strength she'll need to handle whatever happens...*

I must have dozed, because the next thing I knew, I heard the sound of the car door closing. They were home. I waited a few minutes, until Lindsay went upstairs to her room. She was a mess, and I wanted to talk to my mother. I found her in the kitchen, and when I saw her red and swollen eyes, I knew that it was very bad. I feared the answer, but I had to ask. "Mom," I whispered. "What's going on?"

She burst into tears. "It doesn't sound good, Amanda..."

Steve was still in the hospital, and he would remain there for a day or two, hooked up to IVs and a catheter, in the hope that the blockage had been caused by crystals in his urine, but the vets were not confident. It could be bladder stones, and that would mean thousands of dollars' worth of surgery, which we could not afford, or it could be a tumor. "Euthanasia is an option," the vet had said.

Lindsay was devastated, of course. She was lying on her bedroom floor, sobbing uncontrollably. She had bid Steve goodbye, not certain she would ever see him again, and it had taken every ounce of strength she possessed. He was only seven years old. It couldn't be his time.

Tearfully, my mother and I hugged good night. I returned to my room, and to my journal. I am not a religious person, but I do pray when there is nothing else to do, and now I had no choice by to pray as hard as I ever had before, so in desperation, I wrote a brief missive to Saint Francis of Assisi—the patron saint of animals—and to God himself:

Lindsay is a wreck. I feel so terribly for her I want to cry. Please give my sister a miracle. Please don't make her go through this, not now. Steve is too young to die. It isn't time yet. I am begging you, please have mercy and spare my sister this horrible pain. Please don't take Steve.

****

I lay in my bed, but I did not feel any better. The dread that had hung over me all day had not subsided with my prayer, and I felt entirely helpless. It was then that something told me to try again. *God,* I whispered. *If Steve is going to be okay, let me feel peace.* Instantly, I felt peace, and I *knew* that everything would be fine. It was the strangest thing, but I was absolutely certain. As though they were mere vapor, the fear and doubt evaporated: Steve was not going to die. I could go to sleep now; there was no need to worry anymore.

About an hour later, I was awakened by the jangling of the telephone beside my bed, and my heart sank. No one would call us at two-thirty in the morning unless something bad had happened, so it had to be the vet. Who else could it be? I rolled onto my side and curled into a fetal position. I knew for a fact that Lindsay could not go on without Steve, so what if God had ignored my prayers? How would she possibly survive?

I was half-asleep when my bedroom door burst open. "Amanda!" Lindsay's voice was shaking, and I still feared the worst, but when I turned the light on, I saw that her face was filled with pure elation. "Steven's going to be okay!"

I burst into tears and threw my arms around my mother and sister. "I *knew* it!"

The three of us sat on my bed for several minutes, hugging and crying with the sheer happiness of the knowledge that Steve's precious live had been spared. It had indeed been the vet on the phone, but the news was all good: Steve did not have a tumor, there was no sign of bladder stones, and they did not even find crystals in his urine. They now believed he had had a muscle spasm around his urethra, and that it was likely a one-time event--he would need to eat prescription cat food for the rest of his life, but he was expected to make a full recovery.

****

Steve had to stay in the hospital for two more days because he was still hooked up to the catheter, and the vet wanted to wait for him to urinate on his own before releasing him. By all accounts, he was a terrible patient—we were told that he tried to pull his catheter out, he refused to eat, and once the catheter was removed, he waited until the last possible minute to urinate. This was not surprising, as he has always done everything on his own terms and conditions, but when my mother and Lindsay went to pick him up at the hospital, the reunion was nothing less than joyous. A voice on the P.A. system sang out, "Steve's family is here!" The vet tech led them back to the patient area, and right away, Steve recognized the sound of his "mother's" footsteps. Lindsay pulled him into her arms and wept into his soft Creamsicle coat, while he nestled against her shoulder and the warm vibrations of his contented purring washed over them both. Sometimes prayers are answered. Sometimes miracles happen.

20.
The Adopted
Diane Arelle

It started out innocently enough.

"Can we get a dog?"

I stopped drinking my morning coffee and glanced at my oldest child, Kay. Then at I glanced at my husband, Tom, who continued to eat his cereal like he heard nothing.

"I'd like another hamster," Steve my younger son piped up.

Tom continued to eat in silence. We all stared at him. Finally I said. "You know, we've been discussing this dog for two years already."

Tom sighed, the heavy sigh of a man being ambushed once again. "I said, I'll look into it. You just can't get a dog. You have to research what kind to get, what breed would fit the family."

I sighed a heavy sigh as well. "You have been investigating this dog for years. If you don't come up with a pet soon, I'm going to the pound."

Tom relaxed and smiled.

"I mean it this time!" I told him.

The next week at breakfast I looked over at my husband and said, "So, Dear. What kind of dog are we going to get?"

"I didn't have time this week, I'm busy."

"That's all right. But you know now that it's summer and school's out it would be the perfect time to get a pet."

Tom smiled, "Fine, I'll look into it."

I smiled back and all was at peace in our house.

An hour later I called Tom at work and announced. "I'm going to the pound for a kitten."

Tom laughed. "Sure you are, see you for dinner."

In Tom's defense, he never really owned a pet so he grew up without a faithful canine or feline companion. I on the other hand grew up deep in the rural country with many cats in the yard and a wonderfully stupid but faithful beagle. Our children were not alone in wanting a pet. I had always figured on owning a pet once I became a responsible adult with a house and minivan.

I piled the kids into my van, picked up my sister and we all went over to the county animal welfare shelter, commonly referred to as "the pound." Tom didn't believe I'd actually go through with it, but I was determined to get a cute little kitten, you know, something that would grow into a cat, one of those wonderful, independent, demanding your total attention when in the mood creatures I'd always adored.

"Let's get a pure black kitten," I suggested since the last two cats I had owned as a teen were black cats.

"Yeah," both kids exclaimed. They didn't really care about the color; just that Mom was getting them a kitten.

One step through the door of the shelter and my eyes watered from the smells of all those diverse penned up animals. As I walked passed the rows of dogs, my heart just about broke. Almost all of them ran up to the front of the cage and I'm pretty sure barked out the message, "Please take me home, I don't wannna die." They were so cute and so desperate, with their tails wagging and their faces looking hopeful.

I felt tears on my cheeks when we got to the listless dog that just lay there with the hopeless expression of a death row inmate. The sign on his cage read, unadoptable.

"Come on," I rushed the boys past that section.

Then we got to the cats.   Of course they were cooler. Most of them just sat there and watched us as if saying, "Wanna adopt me? Go ahead, see if I care."

We passed cage after cage and I wanted them all, but we all agreed on a black kitten and we were there to find one.

One? We hit the jackpot of black kittens.   There on the bottom cage in the middle of the shelter was an entire family of adorable, puffy, fluffy, playful, wee black kittens.   As I bent to get a closer look, something hit me on the top of my head.

I looked up and saw a gray, striped, tiger tabby with his paw extended all the way out of the cage, as if waving.   He reached out to tap me again.

"Meow!" He exclaimed, excitement transmitting from his soft squeaky voice.   Then he started to purr.   It was so loud.   For a cat with such a quiet voice, he had the loudest purr I'd ever heard.

I studied him.   He studied me.   He was older, about half a year old, his eyes looked a little glassy, but his gaze locked with mine.   "Meow!"

I broke the staring contest and looked down at those beautiful ebony kittens tumbling around, doing their darnedest to be adorable.   "Bye-bye," I said to them and asked the attendant to take the gray kitty out of the wire cage.   Then I took him in my arms. He fit perfectly and purred like a lion, loud and steady. I let the kids pet him and the deal was done.

We'd been chosen and adopted.

On the ride home the kids had allowed me to name him Bonbon and by the time we got Bonbon home, I knew we had a really sick kitten on our hands. I called a vet.   The practical part of me said, "Hey you paid $28 for this cat, take him back and get a healthy one." The emotional part said, "You can't do that. The kids love him and he needs help, not a death sentence."

Besides, Bonbon had picked us, how could we let him down?

I took him to see a vet and almost $300 dollars later we had a cat on the mend.

The shock on Tom's face when he came home that night was a mix of disbelief and horror. "The cat is making funny noises," he pointed out as it rubbed against his legs and began that super loud purring.

"That's the he-likes-you noise," I told him.

We put Bonny in the screened sunroom and I told Tom, "Do not let him in the house. If you let him in he'll become a housecat."

Well, of course Tom heard him crying and let him in. Now, even fifteen years later, whenever my husband complains about something Bonny did to the house, I always point out that he was the one who allowed Bonbon to become a house cat.

We all love Bonbon, and it has been a great decade and a half. Kay has gone off to live in the UK, Steve enjoys taking care of Bonbon and in the evenings Bonny is my lap cat Even Tom has accepted that we are a pet owning family. He feeds the cat most nights if I'm out and calls him in at bedtime.

I never say that Bonbon is a member of our family, because he adopted us at the pound that day. Rather, we are all members of Bonbon's family and we are grateful he chose us.

21.
The Calendar Cat
Judy Brand

I love surprises.   However, I recently had a surprise that made me feel happy and a bit guilty, too.   While browsing in a musty corner of a country antique shop, I was startled to see an image from my early childhood.   This was not simply a familiar image, but an image that I loved even before I could talk, an image that I had only seen on the wall in my great-grandmother's home in the late 1940's.   Suddenly, I realized that my great-grandmother had been missing from my thoughts for a long time.   I was sorry that I had misplaced memories of her, but I was happy to find them again.   Especially, in such an unlikely place.   Although a pungent mildewed aroma tickled my nose, I couldn't move from the area.

As I gazed at the image in front of me, I found my mind racing to relive road trips in the back seat of our green hump-backed Ford, to visit my great-grandmother.   I was quickly lost somewhere between past and present.   Old memories of spring time visits painted my mind.   Berlin, Texas where she lived, was magical in the spring.   Each fertile field was an impressionistic palate of cerulean bluebonnets, orange Indian paintbrush, and pink buttercups.   Hereford bulls appeared to swim through the sea of bluebonnets that filled the pastures.

I was silently laughing about the stacks of bluebonnet photos for sale.   Images of those deep blue flowers became gray bluebonnets when photographed with black and white film, the film of that era.   Suddenly a fragile, sweet voice interrupted my thoughts.   Stunned back into the present, I realized I had missed the tiny lady's question.   Again she asked if I liked Chessie.   Not understanding her inquiry, I answered with a questioning look.

Pointing to the image that decorated the calendar on the wall in front of me, the gentle voice explained that Chessie was the name of the cat on the calendar, a calendar identical to the one that had adorned the wall in my great-grandmother's house.

Chessie was a sleeping gray tabby cat, painted with her head resting comfortably on a pillow. While her paw peeked out from the blanket pulled close to her chin, her partly shut eyes and baby pink nose added to her appeal. More than fifty years after I first saw Chessie, she charmed me for the second time. Excited that I was interested in Chessie, the shop owner mentioned Chessie's hero, Peake. Pointing to another calendar nearby, the lady introduced me to Peake's image. He was a handsome gray and white striped tabby who sat upright, proudly wearing a military hat while he stood at attention.

In the painting, Peake held his head high as he waited for a helmeted officer to hang a medal of honor around his neck. Just below Peake in the painting, Chessie, in her familiar sleeping pose, appeared to be dreaming of her war hero. The year on the calendar was 1945, the year that World War II ended and the year I was born.

The friendly shop keeper explained that Chessie and Peake were created for the highly effective advertising campaign of Chesapeake and Ohio Railway. The images of the sleeping feline and her male cat friend had been successful in capturing the hearts of Americans throughout the country. My mind started churning memories as the lady spoke. As a young child, I often napped at my great-grandmother's house. I always fell asleep with Chessie as my companion, hanging on the wall above my bed. Childhood memories of those visits with my great-grandmother were entwined with memories of Chessie, too. To perpetuate those memories, I purchased the calendar with Chessie and Peake for my home.

As I hung it on the wall, I realized that I knew more about Chessie and Peake than I knew about my great-grandmother. Since she lived less than seven years after my birth, I was forced to turn to aging relatives and the library archives to learn about her life. Many of my questions remain unanswered. I will never know why that tiny, blonde, thirteen year old, named Emilie Mueller boarded a ship in Germany, without her family, to come to the small settlement of New Berlin, Texas, in the 1800's. I will always wonder what happened in her life to encourage her to leave her homeland at such a young age.

I didn't notice that this woman who raised twelve children, planted crops, and tended the farm, never learned to speak English. I remember the joy in her voice each time she held out her arms when I approached. "Udy, Udy," she would say, dropping the "J" from the beginning of my name. I was enchanted by the unique sound of my name as it rolled from her lips. My memory continues to taste the unique flavors that poured from her jars of vegetables. Well into her eighties, my great-grandmother continued to raise her own vegetables and can them herself. She always put one of those colorful jars in my arms when I left her house. As she did, she would point to the jar and say, "Gut, gut," with a smile in her voice. Her sparkling azure eyes were as memorable as the bluebonnets in the fields. As she aged, her eyes continued to dance behind the thick round lenses in her wire rimmed glasses when she spoke to me.

I will never forget Emilie Mueller's vivacity. Chessie will always be there to remind me.

22.
THE CAT WHO STAYED
FOR DINNER
Fred Skolnik

My big mistake was sliding open the patio door when I saw the cat peering into the living room. I figured that would frighten him away but he walked right in, not afraid of me at all, so I imagined he was a neighborhood house cat though he had a wild look and seemed to be challenging me. He made a leisurely circuit of the living room, looking around with apparent interest. I tried to shoo him out but he turned on me and hissed. He was big and gray and didn't look at all like a house cat now, though I had never seen an alley cat behave this way. I took a broom out of the closet and tried to push him toward the patio door but he hissed again and strolled into the kitchen.

I followed him at a certain distance. He made another circuit and then walked right toward me. I stepped aside from the doorway to let him pass. Again I tried to get him out but he ignored my maneuvers and walked toward the stairway. Now I tried to head him off but he hissed again and again I stepped aside. I had a feeling that there was something rational, even thought out, in his movements.

He was upstairs for a quarter of an hour. I waited in the living room, understanding that he was inspecting the house and hoping that when he was finished he might leave. When he came back he meowed at me so I understood he wanted to eat but I was not about to accommodate him, knowing that once you fed a cat he was yours forever. When I ignored him he hissed. I picked up the broom and made a threatening motion. The cat walked away and after a while made himself comfortable on one of the living room chairs.

I didn't know what to do. Usually, under such circumstances, cats went to sleep but this one had a very uncatlike look on his face, as though he was sizing me up. I half expected him to address a few words to me. I watched him for a while and then went into the kitchen to prepare my dinner. This was what I usually did at that hour. I'd never had a wife so I took care of myself and didn't bother much with people.

I figured I'd eat first and then figure out a way to get rid of him, but the moment I sat down he was there, sniffing the air and then jumping up on the table. Instinctively I drew back and the cat dug right in, planting himself at the edge of my plate and not even looking at me. I stood up and took a step back. I was not an assertive type. It occurred to me to pour boiling water on him but I was afraid of how he'd react. If I'd had a gun I might have shot him.

After he finished eating the cat returned to the living room. I was too distraught to sit down. Again I shooed him toward the door with the broom but he didn't move from the chair where he was curled up comfortably. An hour passed, and then another. It was clear he wasn't going anywhere. It struck me as somewhat uncanny that a cat should exercise its will in such a bold and even calculating manner. He must be an extraordinary cat, I thought. My imagination began playing tricks on me too. At one moment I saw him puffed up and magnified like a man-sized figure, at another fierce like a jungle cat.

I left him on the chair and went upstairs, closing the patio door. I had no choice in the matter. In any case it was time to sleep. But after I got into bed I sensed him in the room. I was about to investigate when he leaped onto the bed. I jumped up and retreated a step or two. Then I took a step toward him with my hand raised threateningly and shouted at him to get away. This time he not only hissed but moved toward me aggressively. I backed away. Immediately he curled himself up on my pillow. I thought I saw him jerk his head, as though showing me the door. Again I was at a loss what to do. Certainly I had no intention of remaining in the room with him. I slept in the second bedroom.

In the morning he came down first, waiting for me in the kitchen. Again I had no intention of feeding him. The best tactic, I believed, would be to starve him out. I'd eat my meals in a restaurant and eventually hunger would drive him away. When he saw that I didn't intend to eat or feed him he came toward me in a menacing way, hissing all the while. I understood him perfectly. He might as well have had a gun pointed at me. I went to the refrigerator and tossed him a piece of cheese. Then I retreated into the living room.

The cat came in after a while and looked at me. It was difficult to interpret the look. I sat down but he hissed at me. I understood that he didn't want me sitting in the chair so I got up. It wasn't clear what he wanted. He hissed again and moved toward me. I retreated to the other side of the room and the cat leaped up on the chair and curled up again. When I started to open the patio door he also hissed so I knew he didn't want me to and stopped.

He kept watching me, commenting in his way on everything I did, or rather hissing with varying degrees of intensity when he disapproved and making threatening movements when he was particularly displeased. I got to understanding him very well. In this way we passed another day together and in the night I went straight to the second bedroom.

In the morning I fed him. During the day he ordered me about, hissing and jerking his head. He liked to watch television in the evening and even had his favorite programs. He was as human as anyone could possibly be and I could see that we were going to be together for a long time.

Fred Skolnik is the author of *The Other Shore* (Aqueous Books, 2011), an epic novel depicting Israeli society at a critical juncture in its recent history. His second novel, *Death*, was published by Spuyten Duyvil in 2015. His stories and essays have appeared in over 150 journals, including *TriQuarterly, Gargoyle, The MacGuffin, Los Angeles Review, Prism Review, Words & Images, Literary House Review, Montréal Review, Underground Voices, Third Coast, Word Riot, The Recusant,* and *Polluto*. *Under a pen name, he also published two novels in 2014: Rafi's World and The Links in the Chain.*

23.
THE FULL KITTY
Leigh Lewis

Empty cup?

I drank up.

Empty plate?

I just ate.

Empty lap?

Time to nap!

24.
The Lady or the Cat
Jackie Kingon

Is he who opens a door and he who closes it the same being?
Gaston Bachelard (1884-1962)
French philosopher of science, Sorbonne

Katherine was in a luxury hotel. She sat on a flowery chintz sofa next to a kidney shaped coffee table. Her left hand cradled a green velvet throw pillow. She glanced at a clock on a small brown desk. It said eleven o'clock. Then she stretched her legs encased in leopard colored leggings.

She had spent the morning in the large and mazelike mall that ran under the hotel. She had wandered its twisted hallways for hours trying to find her way back to her room, asking strangers who pointed in different directions making her confused. Then she spotted a familiar looking dull red door. It was hard to push open but when she did she was amazed that it led directly back to her room. How could she have missed it?

She pushed a button on the phone that sent up a bell hop. Immediately as though waiting outside her door a man neither young nor old with brown eyes, wearing a spiffy rust colored jacket that blended well with his cropped hair opened the door and entered. His left breast pocket was covered with an ornate gold script far more appropriate to illustrate the Book of Kells than used for a hotel badge. It was so intricate she couldn't decipher the hotel's name.

She smiled, pointed to her bags and said, "Could you please bring these downstairs and get me a taxi?"

"No," he said.

"No? Then I'll just call the front desk again and ask them to send someone else."

"There is no one else."

"What's your name?"

"Name's Erwin and I'm not a bell hop. There's an in room check-out system; no need to go to the lobby. All one has to do is walk through that door. He pointed behind him.

Katherine looked. She didn't remember the door being so small nor as black as obsidian.

"If you're not here for my bags why are you here? I want to go home."

His eyes crinkled in a devilish twinkle. "And I'm here to help you get home," he said. Then, "You don't know who I am do you?"

The question startled Katherine. Her brow wrinkled. Try as she might she couldn't remember where her home was or who the man was.

Suddenly a sound like a roar from a crowded stadium filled the room.

"What's that?" she said.

"Spectators."

Katherine had no idea what he meant but it didn't matter. It had been deadly quiet until now so what difference did some noise matter; she was leaving. "Here," she said pulling a twenty dollar bill from her wallet, "this should be more than enough for two bags."

Now there were other overlapping whispering like sounds. She strained to make out the words but couldn't. Then she groped for her wallet again flipping her newly washed strawberry blond hair that she had scented with a lemon conditioner in anticipation of her journey home and pulled out another ten. "Look thirty is as high as I go."

"Put your money away. I'm not a bell hop. I'm a facilitator."

She glanced around the room and thumped her chest. "Well facilitator or whatever you are, in case you haven't noticed I'm that person. I'm the only one here."

"Think so? Look in the mirror."

She turned. There was a floor to ceiling mirror on the back wall.

"Where did that come from" she asked. "I would have remembered something as large as that."

Her green eyes narrowed. She walked toward the mirror. Instead of seeing one reflection there were many. The nearest image the largest. The rest trailed down in size looking like a speck in the distance. "Ha! Very funny. Trick mirror."

"It's not a trick, Kitty. Do you mind if I call you Kitty, not Katherine. Katherine is so formal and Kitty is your nickname. Right?"

She drew a blank for a long moment. Then as though a cloud had lifted said, "Kitty, yes. Kitty. Now I remember. That's what everyone at home calls me. But I never liked Kitty. I prefer Katherine."

Erwin crossed his arms sighed and frowned.

Katherine remembered a large luxurious house that was her home. She remembered being pampered yet confined. The pampering part was nice but she chafed at her confinement. The last thing she remembered was being in the garden and picking petals off a daisy that grew near the high wall that surrounded the house and saying the words "in, out, in, out" as each fell to the ground hoping that the last petal would reveal what she should do. Then she remembered seeing a crack in the wall and pushing through. The next thing she knew she was at this hotel.

Erwin gave a sideways smile and cracked his knuckles, a sound she disliked. Instinctively her spine straightened.

Erwin rubbed his finger nails on his shirt. "Besides being a facilitator I'm also a bookie. It's sort of a hobby of mine."

"Bookie? As in placing bets?"

"One and the same."

"Does the money to run this place come from gamblers and you hold your guests hostage until they pay?" She paused eyes narrowing. "Am I a hostage in this hotel or a guest?"

"Depends on your point of view."

He opened the palm of his left hand and put something to his ear and said, "Place your bets. She's at the starting gate."

Katherine asked, "Who's at the starting gate? What are they betting on?"

"The greatest contests are the ones one has with one's self. Wouldn't you agree?" Katherine was not sure what he meant so she said nothing. She peered in the mirror again and now saw what looked like thousands of reflections of herself. She jerked backward so quickly she almost fell.

Erwin came closer. "No one knows which one of you will survive and get the opportunity to go home."

No sooner did she say "But those are reflections" than the glass wall became misty and soft like gauze.

"Think so," spat a voice that sounded exactly like hers.

"Who said that?" Katherine cried. The mirror rippled like a piece of wet silk fluttering in a breeze. She peered closer. Suddenly a hand extended through the mirror and grabbed her arm.

"Who's the illusion you or me?

The hand felt warm.

Her arteries and veins expanded in terror.

A chorus sounded, "Who's the illusion? Who's the illusion?"

Then without any feelings of transition she was on the other side of the mirror and looking straight into the eyes of the other Katherine her fists clenched and unclenched, the urge to scratch overwhelming. She looked at her hands. Had her nails always been so long?

Her double watched and hissed.

They were suspended in the middle of a great sphere standing on a point of light.   Swollen bubbles of color, violet, turquoise, silver, orange, like arms of a lacy galaxy swirled through them.

They each touched themselves.   Then touched the other. Solid.   They both felt solid.   They both took a step back gawked and froze.   They were more identical than the closest identical twins right down to a tiny scar over the right eyebrow something that happened when Katherine was a child and fell chasing a ball.

Katherine's double repeated, "Who's the illusion, you or me?"

A trumpet fan fared.

A voice that came from everywhere at once said, "Diagnostics completed.   Restraints deactivated.   Welcome to the arena."

Katherine saw Erwin behind a glass who made a thumb up. A large clock suspended over his head was counting down from sixty seconds.

Katherine's voice quivered.   "What happens now?" she said to her duplicate.

"We fight."

"Why would I want to fight you?"

"We all fight ourselves from time to time just not so literally." She gave Katherine a significant shove.   Her claw like nails scratched into her arm and left an oozing bright red line.

Katherine screamed. The clock had twenty seconds left. It was one thing to fight a stranger in self-defense and another to fight an identical self. "How far does this have to go?"

"Till there is only one of us."

"Why only one of us?"

"The doorway was built for only one."

"And all the rest?"

"They collapse; they are cancelled."

"Meaning?"

"It's the law of the quantum. She made a circular motion with her arm. All the other Katherine's who had stood in a descending line zoomed closer appearing like smeared waves of colors rippling around her. "You have to kill me and all of them," she said.

"I can't kill you." Katherine's voice rose. "I can't." She gulped. Her mouth felt dry. She coughed. She looked at the other Katherine waiting to make a move. "What if I do nothing?"

"Doing nothing is doing something." She paused so Katherine could feel the enormity of what she had just said. "We all want to get home." She shoved and scratched her again. This time the shove was much harder. The scratch much deeper.

The clock struck zero."

A drum roll sounded. A chorus chanted, "Fight, Fight, Fight."

Katherine put one hand in front of her face to protect it. The other she thrust forward making a connection with the other Katherine's jaw. She jiggled around. She felt more confident. She struck her again.

The other Katherine's head snapped back. She steadied herself. Then with renewed force gave Katherine a one-two: a punch in the solar plexus followed by an upper cut. Katherine flipped into the air, rolled twice and fell. She plunged through an explosion of glowing fragments; felt a scissoring pain from broken ribs. The floor cleared beneath her vision. She lay face upward, awareness suspended. Then her eyes rolled up in her head. Silence.

The crowd roared. Lights blinked. A bell rang.

Next moment she was standing in the center of the great sphere again facing another Katherine feeling perplexed but refreshed. But which one was she: the one who fell or the one left standing? She only knew she had returned to the starting point.

She inhaled deeply. Blinked. Then...

WHACK! Fragments of time and space twisted and crashed through her like frames of a revolving door. Again and again and again and again. Faster and faster and faster.

Each altercation cancelled one Katherine out of existence. No feeling of near or far. No feeling of up or down. A sequence of colors bled into each other and blurred into white light. The cheering so loud it became white sound. Again and again and again.

And then it was over.

Katherine was back in the hotel room but she didn't know if she was in the same hotel or had slipped through a different mirror into another hotel room in another universe. Did it matter? Play the hand you're dealt, she thought. She waited for a clue to help her know how to react. She saw that the mirror had shrunk but the front door had grown. It was brown with an old fashioned glass doorknob. She though she saw one like it before.

Erwin sat on the edge of the bed that someone had carefully made up and covered with a green and white striped bedspread. Was it new? Who had put it there?

"Well done, Kitty," he said. "Oh excuse me, I meant to say Katherine but Kitty seems so right. All of my associates are delighted. You didn't disappoint us."

Erwin prodded, "Now do you remember the name of the hotel?"

Katherine thought but still could not remember. Her breath was quick and shallow. She was warm. She was wearing a fur coat. Why was she wearing it? When had she bought it? When had she put it on? She squirmed to remove it but it seemed to grow from her skin. She shook and steadied herself.

"The hotel is called The Copenhagen," he laughed. "For some that is the home of great aquavit, best smorgasbord and herring."

Herring? Katherine's mouth watered. She licked her lips.

"Also quantum experiments; but in your case it's also known as the lost and found."

Katherine said nothing.

"When you wandered from our home my friends bet that I wouldn't be able to find you. You see there is a law that says that it is not possible for me to measure speed and position at the same time. You were lucky I figured this box would be the most logical place for you to go."

Katherine narrowed her eyes. Was she in a Chinese puzzle box: a box within a box within a box?

"My complete name is Erwin Rudolf Josef Alexander Schrödinger. Does that mean anything to you?"

"Should it?" she said.

"We had a close relationship."

Katherine studied Erwin. She took a cautious step away. He wasn't the least bit attractive to her. "Why was I put through such an ordeal?"

"I'm sorry it was an ordeal. It was supposed to be more like a heavy workout at a gym.

Something to toughen you up. Make you the best version of yourself that you can possibly be."

"Yeah, well, you weren't the one doing the fighting."

"But here you are. Not even a scratch. All ready for the final contest."

"Final contest?

There was a distant cheering. Katherine instinctively covered her ears with her hands and cringed. Would she never get home? She felt like Alice in the Red Queen's race: running in place.

Erwin ran his hand through his hair. "I also rescue cats who have wandered into the box that technically makes them dead and alive at the same time."

"That's impossible. Didn't Einstein say God doesn't play dice with the universe?

Erwin's eyes widened. "I didn't know you were listening when my friends and I discussed such things. Let's just say, God works in mysterious ways."

"Why a cat? Why not a chicken?"

Erwin thought of a chicken and laughed. "I like cats and you were handy."

Katherine grew anxious. "Is this some kind of a lady and a tiger thing where one door has a lady and one a tiger?"

"Something like that. Maybe."

"Maybe? All of this seems to be about maybe."

"It is," he laughed. "You know, you are a remarkable creature about to make history." His cell phone rang. "Yes, yes," he said into it. "Last and final contest about to begin. Just need one more moment."

Katherine watched him glance at the clock. It was eleven fifty five. Erwin said, "You have to check out at twelve. You have five minutes. Then this room is automatically sterilized so it can be used again."

At first Katherine remained very still. Then she arched her back and shifted from one foot to the other.

"Would you like something to drink?" Erwin asked. He walked to the small bar in the corner of the room, opened a refrigerator and took out a saucer of milk that looked like it had been waiting to be retrieved and put it on the floor next to the bar. "Here Kitty Kitty," he said. "Here Kitty Katherine."

She walked toward the bar. Was she growing smaller or was the bar growing larger? Did it matter? She wanted the milk. She lowered her head and tasted with her tongue. Then she lapped until it was gone.

"Better?" Erwin said.

Her mind cleared.

Erwin leaned down and took her in his arms. His fingers stroked her throat. "Chin up, Kitty" he said.

He walked to the door, turned the doorknob and peered into the darkness.

"Is there no other way?" she purred.

"No. No other way. No other way home."

"Will I know when I get there?"

"Maybe," he smiled. "Depends."

Katherine paused and looked at Erwin. "Go on, go on," Erwin urged.

There was a tiny drop of milk on the back of her hand. She licked it off then walked through the doorway. "Meow," she said turning to take a momentary glance backward, a last look at Erwin. "Meow," she said louder hearing the door click behind.

25.
THE MAN WHO DIDN'T LIKE CATS
Frank Roger

1

As Herbert came home from work and slammed the door shut behind him, he saw from the corner of his eye how a familiar black shape leapt out of the window, and thus out of his range of vision.

Damned creature, he thought, anger welling up inside him. He put down his briefcase and hurried to the window the black shape had escaped through. So old Mrs. Clarence's cat had gained entry to his apartment once again. Dammit, he thought, what has the creature been up to this time? He quickly completed a tour of inspection of his apartment. Yes, indeed, as he could have guessed the wretched animal hadn't spent its time idly here, hadn't limited itself to casual sightseeing. Not that he expected anything but trouble from the black monster.

He cursed when he noted a curtain had been torn, a wire connecting his stereo rig had been bitten through and a cushion on his couch was spreading the distinct odour of cat's urine. He hated the damned cat - and judging from its activities in his apartment during his absence, the feelings were very much mutual.

He considered his options.

One : go and talk about the problem with Mrs. Clarence.

Two : go and talk about the problem with the landlord.

Three : to hell with the old bitch one floor down and the not-so-old-but-equally-hopeless man two floors down and take drastic measures himself.

The first option had little going for it, he realised. Mrs. Clarence kept repeating that cats were extremely careful and clean and easily house-trained animals, and that her cat in particular would never do the horrible things Herbert accused it of. Knocking down glasses and vases and messing up his rooms? Urinating on the couch? Ripping curtains and blankets and clothes to shreds? Out of the question! The poor animal never even left her own apartment, so where did he get the idea it was responsible for all that went wrong over at his place? No doubt he was just looking for a scapegoat to blame everything on : his ramshackle equipment that kept breaking down, his worn-out clothes and stuff, the leaks in the ceiling and his own spilled drinks forming puddles everywhere. He ought to get his act together, and stop drinking and imagining things, instead of blaming a poor woman's innocent cat, her only companion and solace in the loneliness of old age. He ought to be ashamed of himself.

Discussions with the landlord, who lived down on the first floor, tended to lead to absolutely nothing as well. Yes, the man invariably replied, nodding in agreement, there was no need to remind him of the fact that the tenants were not allowed to keep pets, he knew very well it was explicitly stated in the contract, and yes, he would definitely talk about it with Mrs. Clarence, and settle the matter once and for all. No pets were allowed and there was no reason whatsoever to make an exception for the old woman's cat. But of course the man never broached the subject with the woman on the second floor, or if he did his efforts remained without effect. Probably the man was one of those goddamned cat lovers himself and didn't really mind Mrs. Clarence keeping a pet, even if it was against the rules, and presumably he didn't want to admit to Herbert that he was giving the old woman some leeway in this respect, considering the fact she had lost her husband a long time ago and didn't he understand she needed the company and comfort only the heart-warming presence of a cat could provide? Anyway, cats were harmless creatures, so why would they take away what was essential for Mrs. Clarence's happiness and well-being, and so forth and so on.

That left him with option number three. He would start work on a strategy soon. It wouldn't be easy, he would have to be extremely careful, and a wide variety of elements had to be taken into account, but it should be possible to work out a plan with a reasonable chance of success.

2

One night's sleep would be well worth the sacrifice, provided his second stratagem proved more successful than his first attempt at cat hunting. The dish of poisoned cat food he had left on the floor, close to the window left invitingly ajar, hadn't been touched - although there were traces of a nightly cat's visit. It was as if the damn creature had wanted to make it clear to him that his attempt at poisoning it were totally ridiculous and absolutely futile. It had knocked down a few baubles on his bookcase, slid a magazine from his coffee-table onto the floor, and left a latticework of scratches on his fake mahogany desk, like signatures in a visitors' book, proving at once it had put in an appearance and found, examined and rejected the poisoned food. Herbert knew cats were choosy and had a highly developed olfactory sense, so he had opted for a colourless, odourless and tasteless poison. It hadn't fooled the cat, however.

So this time he had prepared a dish of pure cat food, not tampered with in any way, totally harmless. He had even added a few extra ingredients he knew cats were very fond of. This gourmet cat meal should be absolutely irresistible to any normal cat. Only this time he would be waiting for the uninvited (but not unexpected) guest - armed with a spraycan that should blind the creature and turn it into a helpless prey. He would be out of sight, yet close enough for the fatal blow. He had rehearsed the ambush and his subsequent attack a few times in his mind, had tried to foresee what could possibly go wrong and how to remedy those shortcomings in his strategy. He was convinced he hadn't overlooked the slightest detail and success could not elude him anymore.

So he waited, darkness completely enveloping him, with only the sounds of the night coming through the open window rupturing the peace and tranquillity. Time went by. The cat didn't show its face. Herbert forced himself to stay awake, and remain motionless and silent in his hiding place. Every now and then he took a sip from his bottle. More time went by. The night seemed endless, a period of absolute emptiness stretching into infinity. He didn't care how long he would have to wait. All that mattered now was the realisation of his objective : getting his hands on the cat and finishing it. Yet more time went by, teasingly slow.

Dammit, he thought, suddenly alarmed. He must have dozed off for a while there, because now he could see the first signs of approaching dawn in the night sky, and the last moment he remembered it had still been completely dark. He shook his head, casting off the sleep threatening to jeopardise his mission. He took another sip from his bottle, noticed it was half empty. Was the drink perhaps responsible for his dozing off? Impossible. He had been known to drink more of the stuff without growing sleepy. He was quite used to a little liquor; maybe he simply hadn't slept enough the past few days. As the night slowly turned into morning and the darkness dissipated, he noticed the cat food had been eaten. The dish was empty, had even been licked clean. A wave of despair washed over him. Had it been pure bad luck that the cat had entered his apartment when he had dozed off for a few minutes? Or, he hated the very idea, had the cat been patiently waiting outside for exactly that to happen, then rushed inside at the proper moment, gobbled up the delicious meal he had prepared, and left without a trace?

Well, not quite without a trace, he remarked as he noted the little puddle of what could only be cat's piss... right in front of him, within reaching distance. Frustratingly close to his hands. He threw the spray can aside, rose to his feet, tried to loosen up his cramped muscles. He looked at his watch: still an hour and a half before he had to go to work. He would try to get some sleep before he left. And try to come up with a better method to get rid of his mortal enemy. Something told him that wouldn't be so easy. He had underestimated his enemy once, but that wouldn't happen twice.

He would make sure the third blow would be the fatal one.

3

Herbert yawned. Catching up on sleep might be a good idea for tonight. He had prepared a quick dinner, downed a few drinks (well, more than just a few, to be honest), watched TV for about fifteen minutes, and decided to call it a day. All his plans would have to wait - and that included the Great Plan To Solve The Cat Problem Once And For All.

So he retired to bed early, determined to let nothing get in the way of a good night's sleep.

Only he hadn't counted on one contender in the great man versus feline sweepstakes, he realised as he heard the meowing in his living room. At first he decided to ignore the damn cat. He needed his sleep, and anyway he hadn't worked out his tactics for his final and decisive onslaught yet. He would let the cat get away with one more nightly rampage, if grudgingly.

But the meowing grew increasingly persistent, and when he heard the sound of a vase that was knocked down to the ground and ended up shattered into a million fragments, he knew he was being called to battle. Sleep seemed to recede into the distance; it would have to wait until this matter had been settled. There was no way he could afford not to rise to this challenge. More disturbing sounds, coming from his living room, reached his ears. He worked himself into an upright position, sighed deeply, and cast off the last vestiges of sleep. He just had to pick up the gauntlet. Sleep would be his reward, when he returned victorious from the battlefield. A good night's sleep, and waking up in the knowledge that no unwelcome visitors would ever invade his privacy and do unnameable things during his absence again. He gathered his strength and jumped out of his bed, ready for action. He would show no mercy.

His living room was shrouded in semi-darkness, transformed into an eerily shimmering chiaroscuro each time the clouds obscuring the moon parted and allowed the moonlight to blend with the pale shine of the street lights spilling into the room through the windows. For a moment Herbert considered switching on the light, but decided against it. A well-lit room might make it easy for him to follow the cat's movements, but it would be a distinct disadvantage in that the cat would also clearly see him. It would have no trouble parrying his (sadly unprepared) attacks.

He waited for his eyes to adjust to the murk, then stepped forward, casting glances in all directions, concentrating on any sound that might help him in determining the cat's whereabouts. Silence was complete. Had he dreamed the cat was roaming around here? That would seem hardly likely. He bumped into his coffee-table, and an empty glass clattered to the ground. There was no reaction. The cat should have been at least as startled as he and should have yelped at the crash so unexpectedly rupturing the silence. Still, there had been nothing. Clearly, the cat must have left. Or had never been in here to start with. He was about to return to his bedroom when he heard the meowing in his kitchen.

He quickly strode into the kitchen, fury welling up inside him. In here it was completely dark; no light spilled this far inside his apartment. There! Cat's eyes. Cats did have red eyes, didn't they? Or... was it merely some reddish glow or reflection, a fluorescence on a display panel on some of his electronic kitchen equipment? There was no way to tell, of course. But the cat just had to be here. He'd heard the damn creature. But right now he neither heard nor saw a thing. No doubt it was hiding someplace, closely watching him, preparing its next move.

He cursed as he heard a shriek and a series of dull thuds coming from his living room. The damn cat was driving him crazy. Was it doing this on purpose, in an effort to send him into a raging fury and render his attack less effective? He would have to control his emotions, keep himself in check, and stay level-headed, or he wouldn't stand a chance against this agile and quick-witted opponent.

He rushed back into the living room, thought he saw a black shape move towards his bookcase, and darted in that direction. Before he could get there, he tripped over the empty glass lying on the floor, smacked his knee painfully into the coffee-table and went down, thrashing wildly about. He tried to hold on to what appeared to be a line of books, which came crashing down onto him. He lay there for a while, sprawling, gasping for breath, recovering from the shower of books and baubles that had hit him. The throbbing pain in his knee made him crawl into an upright position and take stock of his admittedly rather deplorable situation. He tried to ignore the pain and rose to his feet, his face a contorted mask of fury and frustration. There was no way he would let the cat get away with this. He would not allow it to get the upper hand. Or paw.

He leaned rather heavily against the bookcase, and more books came tumbling down. He steadied himself, knocked a few more baubles down and froze when he heard the cat meowing, clearly now, unmistakably, mockingly. The creature was enjoying its successes. He would make sure its joy would be short-lived.

A dimly visible black shape darted between his wobbly legs, and, completely taken by surprise, he lashed out at it, lost his balance and struck the only bookcase still standing. Another paperback cascade was the result. Furious now, he cursed and slammed his hand against the wall. The cat was teasing him, playing with him as if he were a mouse, wearing him out as a matador would a bull. A long drawn-out meowing filled the room... or was that the sound of squealing tires on the street outside? One moment he was confused. The two sounds were so damn similar. He would have to listen very carefully. If he mistook sounds coming from outside for the cat's noise, it might foul up his plan of action.

There! The black shape had passed before the window, and it had definitely possessed the forms of a cat. It had only been a glimpse, of course, but he was pretty sure he'd seen a cat outlined against the backdrop of the night sky, faintly illuminated by the street lights. He blinked a few times, tried to see more clearly. His vision got rather blurry at times, and his legs grew more wobbly with each passing moment. Of course, he badly needed sleep. And maybe he shouldn't have drunk that much. But how was he to know this night would be the Night of the Battle? Anyhow, it was now too late to change any of that. He had a job to finish here. Better get it over with fast, so he could get back to bed.

He kicked a pile of paperbacks aside, and nearly fell down as he saw the black shape darting past once again. This time he reacted promptly. He hacked and slashed, but only hit thin air. The sound of objects tumbling down to the floor reached his ears... or were those sounds coming from outside again? Never mind all that now. He had to concentrate and ignore any distractions that might interfere with the job at hand.

When he noticed two reddishly glowing eyes in front of him (or were they rather greenish? hard to tell, the colour shimmered, seemed to change hue constantly), mocking him, teasing him, defying him, he lunged forward and started kicking and tearing and hitting everything that came within range. If you're not a sharpshooter, you might as well produce a shower of lead shot you couldn't miss your target with. He cut his hand on something, and pain flashed through his arm and went straight up to his brain. It infuriated him, drove him into a frenzy that made him forget the pain and allowed him to intensify his mad thrashing and milling.

At that point everything became a blur, a whirlpool of sensations perceived too vaguely to fully register, a wildly spinning vortex of shrill sounds, amorphous shapes dimly visible through the murky twilight, acrid smells and sudden jolts of pain. His apartment seemed to flicker in and out of existence, as he caromed from wall to wall, splintering furniture he found on his path, ripping like a tornado through his books and CDs, a puppet whose strings were pulled by a puppet master torn apart by spasms, a wrecking ball swung by a seizure-stricken demolisher. I'm dreaming all this, he thought in a far corner of his mind where a fragment of cold reason still lingered. This is a terrible nightmare. I must be delirious. This can't be real.

It was a relief to feel the cool night air, the sense of total freedom as he felt himself floating, freed of everything that bound him, detached from the real world that had seemed so suffocating just there. Floating. Or was it falling?

Epilogue

Clipping from the <u>Westport Gazette</u>, April 14th, xxxx:

"Yesterday morning Mr Herbert Carruthers was found dead on the sidewalk in front of 47 Coverdale Street, where he lived in his apartment on the second floor. The man apparently fell off his balcony at night, although there are indications he may have been pushed. The autopsy will doubtlessly shed some light on the actual cause of death. It has been confirmed by a reliable source that Mr Carruther's apartment was trashed, although it is as yet unclear whether burglars were involved or if the victim inflicted the damage himself prior to his fatal fall. His downstairs neighbour, Mrs. R.C., told us confidentially that Mr Carruthers had a drinking problem which "may well have been responsible for whatever happened on that fateful night." She added, "He was a strange man. Always complaining, always blaming others for his own blundering. He really shouldn't have drunk so much." Despite this rather harsh criticism, Mrs. R.C. appeared quite smitten with grief at the death of her upstairs neighbour, her voice on the verge of breakdown, tears welling up in her eyes, her cat clutched against her bosom. The sight of the cat, gently purring, with a defiant and even triumphant look in its eyes, clashed rather vehemently with the overall atmosphere of mourning."

26.
The Story of Sam
Stella M. Wissner

In the late summer I noticed a pretty grey tabby cat around my studio in Decatur. The cat had no collar and was shy and scared of people. I put out some food, which was gratefully consumed and kitty eyed me warily from a distance.

I asked Jon who lives in the apartment behind the studio

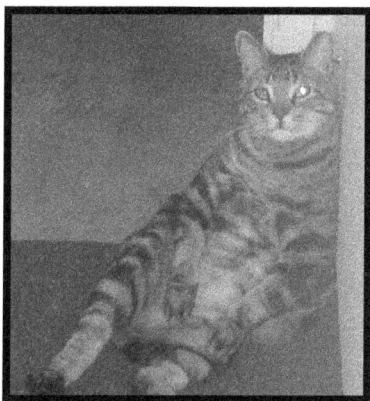

about the cat. He told me that he believed this was the mother cat which had had two kittens under the house in the previous June. One of those kittens, the small sickly black and white one, he had cared for and adopted and called Moon. The other one, a tabby, I took home with me and he became the fourth feline in our household. He is a Great Cat and so we called him Alexander. The stray cat looked just like him. Over the next several months, Momma as we had decided to call her, started to live around the house. Jon fed her in the evenings when he came home from work and I fed her during the day. I noticed evidence of a hard life. There was a piece missing from her ear and she was frequently bloodied. One of her eyes wasn't quite right, we suspected she might be blind in it, as when the other eye was scratched and swollen she didn't seem able to see.

Every morning when I arrived she would be sitting on Jon's doormat in the sun waiting for someone to come. She was desperate for attention and would roll over and play when she'd eaten her food, as long as you didn't come too close. Once again I became very concerned about the future of this cat, which was probably Alexander's Momma, just as I had with Alexander. We could feed her but we were on a very busy street and winter was coming. And we definitely did not need any more kittens to try to find homes for. It started to get cold and Jon built an insulated box for her to sleep in with a blanket but she clearly had eyes on the house. However Jon was worried that she might have ringworm and would re-infect his cats, Moon and Croix so he did not want to let her into the apartment.

I thought about it and decided that the best thing I could do for Momma was to get her fixed, which would increase her chances of survival. Jon and I talked about it and decided that we would try to catch her and take her to the local Humane Society who had agreed to neuter her for a donation and give her shots. Jon and I would then try to find a home for her.

We caught her and I drove her to the Humane Society. She was very good in the car and settled down well. The vet called me the next day with surprising news! "She" was in fact a neutered male, about three years old and quite healthy!! He was blind in one eye but the vet thought it was genetic rather than caused by an accident. So although this cat was around when the kittens were born he wasn't Mom and probably not even Dad! We'll never know but now the issue of a good home became pressing. Neither Jon nor I could take any more cats, we were both at capacity. We told everyone we knew about the cat and advertised on Craig's list all to no avail. I suppose with all his problems he wasn't that appealing, although he is really quite handsome. Memories of my vet saying, "Do you know how hard it is to place a cat?" came to my mind. Jon was still caring for him as well as he could but temperatures were in the 20's and we were getting desperate.

Then a wonderful thing happened. Jon's sister's colleague, Cynthia had lost her cat at Thanksgiving and was quite devastated. She agreed to come and look at Momma's Boy as we were now calling him! She was a large, calm, lovely lady, who worked with troubled kids. We told her the whole story. She came and saw him and agreed to take him. I asked her what she would call him. "I am going to call him Sam" she said, "because it means a gift from God" A lump came up in my throat. That is one lucky little cat I thought, he has found the perfect home and she has a found another treasure.

Stella Wissner is a retired Research Chemist and animal lover living in Atlanta, Georgia with her husband and three cats, Simba an orange tabby, Alexander a brown tabby and Sylvia a long haired silver tabby. All the cats were strays looking for a good home and found them! Stella is an avid gardener and nature lover, a Master birder and sculptor.

Stella started writing short stories about interesting things in her life about ten years ago and now has quite a collection. She writes whenever something happens that she wants to capture. Many of the stories are about cats who are so close to her heart.

27.
THE VIEW
Eleanor Kedney

Peaches ripen on the tree outside.
Silver-blue light dims the late morning glow.
A two-year-old cat sits in a window and watches
cardinals flit among hedges. She's just eaten,
and licked her paws clean. At three o'clock
a woman who answered the ad will come
and take the cat. The girl can no longer keep her.
Silence roves the small apartment. Two
bananas in a bowl have darkened and grown soft.
Their sweetness plumes the air. Both the girl and cat
are sleepy now. What strikes me is the way
the cat nuzzles the girl's thumb, and the girl sings
a lullaby refrain over the cat's purrs. I'll pause
for them—the girl strokes the cat's black ears,
the trust it shows, rolling onto its back.

The rain begins, droplets one-by-one faint
on the glass. Streaks like claw marks blur the view—
torn leaves, a few peaches fallen on the wet ground.
A moment passes, and then the next, while the rain stops,
and birds collect in high branches and break
into song.

Eleanor Kedney is the founder of *The Writers Studio Tucson*, a branch of the New York-based Writers Studio, and served as the Director and the advanced workshop teacher for ten years. Her poems have appeared or are forthcoming in various U.S. and international periodicals, including *Connecticut River Review, Cumberland River Review, Many Mountains Moving, Miramar Poetry Journal, Mslexia, NY Quarterly, San Pedro River Review, and The Maynard*, among other journals. Her work has contributed to the anthology, No Achilles: War Poetry (WaterWood Press, 2015). Her chapbook, The Offering, will be published by Liquid Light Press (2016). She lives with her husband, Peter, dog, Charlie, and cat, Ivy, in Tucson, Arizona and Stonington, Connecticut.

28.
Toonsie to the Rescue
Lynn Maddalena Menna

To paraphrase Mick Jagger, you probably don't know what you want, and it doesn't matter anyway because you'll always get what you need. And sometimes what you need has fluffy black fur, lime-green eyes, and meows.

Whoever said that cats are aloof and independent must have been a dog owner, because Toonsie was high-maintenance. Little did I know that when a cat came running up to me in my yard, she would come to rule the roost. Once Toonsie maneuvered herself into our home, she became the proverbial only child. She demanded, and received, our undivided attention. Prospero and I rearranged our schedules to meet her needs. All meals were planned to include foods that Toonsie enjoyed, with a special emphasis on sushi from her favorite Japanese restaurant. And most importantly, we never, ever attempted to take another vacation once she became a member of our family.

Occasionally, however, we humans do have to have to treat ourselves to a good time, even if it means incurring her wrath.

Toonsie always knew when something was up that might upset her daily routine, so when she constantly meowed on that sunny summer morning, we thought she was protesting our decision to spend the day at the Jersey shore. Being left alone for six hours is animal cruelty in her eyes. But she usually reacted by sitting in the middle of the living room floor and turning her back to us--the ultimate snub.

This day was different. Toonsie was making a racket in the hallway that led to the bedrooms. The crying and meowing was nonstop. Finally, she decided to stick her nose in the electrical outlet. At first I thought it merely was a shameless bid for attention. Toonsie always tended to be a bit dramatic. But then my husband, Prospero, joined her on the floor and stuck his nose near the outlet too. What can I say? He always indulged her.

"I need a screwdriver," he said. At this point I felt like I needed a screwdriver, but not the tool. Prospero removed the switch plate only to find a spark arcing from the outlet. He raced downstairs to shut off the circuit-breaker, thus preventing an electrical fire.

Had it not been for Toonsie's keen sense of smell, we would have returned from our day at the beach only to find our house burned to the ground. More importantly, our precious little cat would have been trapped in the inferno, and our hearts would have been broken forever.

Toonsie wasn't throwing a tantrum on that warm summer morning, she was warning us of danger. I still cannot believe that a little stray kitty cat—that we weren't sure about taking in— prevented a life-changing catastrophe. And as we came to know over and over again, we needed her just as much as she needed us.

Thank goodness for our fuzzy lifesaver. Toonsie saved the day.

29.
Trapped
Diane Payne

The first morning after the cat has escaped; the neighbor girl tells you she couldn't sleep because she heard you calling "Maggie" all night long. You went to bed at eleven, so technically, it wasn't all night long. But you say nothing.

At ten, you sat outside, covered with black cats, black cats that wanted to be with you, unlike your black cat that was probably watching all the other black cats sitting on your lap, becoming even more agitated.

The pet sitter was horrified to discover Maggie had escaped. Technically, Maggie was in the carport shortly after you arrived home, but she wouldn't come inside the house. You'd go to pick her up, she'd take off running. You'd follow her. She'd turn head and scowl, angry you had left town.

Maggie has been living with you for seven months, but this was the first time you have spent a night away from home. Thinking about this, you feel a bit like a loser. Not one night away from home in seven months? What's happening? Are you turning into one of *those* people? You were only gone three nights. There were three other cats and two dogs home. *They* knew you'd return. Maggie has never been an easy cat. Took months of sitting in the hot carport, covered with fleas and mosquitoes, as you fed her and her kittens, trying to coax them inside so you could bring them to get neutered and spayed. Once you finally got the cats in the house, Maggie would jump through the screen, then return the same way she left. Day after day, you'd fix the screen and the neighbors would comment on how you were getting good at repairing screens.

A friend tells you to quit looking because she'll return on her own. The advice sounds plausible, but doing nothing seems reckless, irresponsible.   Neighbors are tired of seeing you peering in their yards, their carports, hearing you scream her name, and they say the same thing: "Your cat will come home." They want *you* gone.

One neighbor tells how someone shot his black cat with a pellet gun. "Cost over six hundred bucks at vet and she still has pellets in her leg."

Another neighbor says maybe your black cat was the one sitting on her golf cart. She shooed it away. "Too many damn cats running around here."

Another friend says: once a feral cat, always a feral cat. "Probably screwing her brains out under a shed."

"She's spayed."

"Screwing for fun then."

On the third day of her absence, you borrow a trap. Get serious. The phone rings. Long distance lover calls. You update him about your trip to Boston. Maggie. He's planning on visiting for a week in a few days. You think you see Maggie and say you'll call him back. "Wait. Don't go!" He sounds urgent. You listen. He tells you that you have too many pets and he's tired of the long distance relationship. He doesn't admit that he has found a new lover.

Asshole.

You get up all night and release five cats from traps. Two cats are in trap last time you empty it. You let the calico free, but aren't sure that black cat hissing at you isn't Maggie. You need to see if the tail is crooked. It's not. The cat races across the street where the kind neighbor feeds all the strays. These cats won't return to your yard.

You hurry home from work, come home at lunch, never leave the neighborhood. Always looking for cat. It's you who is trapped. Maggie is probably having way more fun. Maybe she has found a lover, one without so many damn humans in his life.

After four days of not seeing Maggie, your daughter who is home for spring break, sees the cat out in the yard, the cat she's never been able to pet. Not once in seven months. You go after Maggie and she returns to where you first saw her last summer, under the next-door neighbor's shed. You grab your glass of wine figuring it may take a while, and try to coax her out with the salmon you made for dinner. She grabs a bit, retreats. You ask your daughter to grill a salmon filet for Maggie. Your daughter groans. "You spoil her." You hand her your glass for a refill. She brings the salmon and a glass of wine for herself. She grudgingly hands you your glass and laughs when you swallow the fly, then rip your shorts on a nail. The neighbors wonder if you will ever get the cat and leave their yard. "You can watch our tomatoes grow," neighbor says uncomfortably. You drink more wine. Daughter tweets about your stupidity. Neighbors shut their window, protecting their children from your drunken cat fiasco.

It gets dark. You set up trap, certain you'll catch her. You return home for refills of wine. Put on warm coats. You hear Maggie check out trap. But she's seen that trap filled with cats in your carport. She's not *that* hungry or stupid. When the wine is finished, daughter grows bored. She goes home for a shower. Eventually, you go home. Fifteen minutes later, the salmon is gone, trap has been released, and cat is running free.

Damn cat.

Four hours later, your daughter goes to bed, you put the other three cats in her room, dogs in your room, prop kitchen door open, sit in the dark, and Maggie walks inside the kitchen as if she's never been away.

During the night, she jumps on the bed, just like she has the past seven months. The other cats move over a bit. You open the window. Hot beneath the cats. Is this what the lover didn't enjoy?

Asshole.

Next morning, daughter is finally able to pet Maggie. "She's soft. I'm surprised."

Walking the dogs the next day, you and daughter get caught in a thunderstorm. Return home, find porch door blown wide open. "Oh, no!" you both screech. Maggie is cowered beneath the couch. No interest in leaving, especially in a storm. You both sigh with relief.

Your daughter packs her suitcase for spring break trip. "This weekend home has been nothing but Maggie. Damn cat."

Maggie jumps on the chair and looks triumphant.

30.
Two Cats

Winston Plowes

My cats groom themselves
Vain contortionist coiffeurs
Lick fur... Content purr

Both my cats hunt mice
Miniature jungle tigers
Keep still... Torture, kill

My cats sleep all day
Long symmetrical slumbers
Squashed tail... piercing wail

Both my cats climb trees
Lofty feline ascenders
Scots Pine... 999

My cats play with string
Junior Gladiators
Too fast...Elastoplast

Both my cats eat grass
In creep regurgitators
Retch, wowl... kitchen towel

My cats have been ill
White coat investigators
Nothing found... £100

Winston Plowes lives aboard his floating home with his cat, *Fatty* in the north of England. In the past year he has collaborated with *The Arvon Foundation, the BBC, Glastonbury Festival, UCLAN and Manchester Museum.* He regularly tutors for *The Square Chapel*, Halifax and in schools. Winston was *Poet in Residence* for the *Rochdale Canal Festival* in 2012 and *The Hebden Bridge Arts Festival* 2012-14. Jointly self-published in *Misery Begins at Home*, 2010 and micro Chapbook *Extras*, 2014. His first solo collection of surrealist poetry *Telephones, Love Hearts & Jellyfish, Electric Press* is out this fall. Winston is also inventor of the world's first (and possibly last) *Random Poetry Generating Bicycle, The Spoke-n-Word*.

www.winstonplowes.co.uk

31.
Wants
Christopher Woods

From the window, moon glow showers the room. Inside that room, inside a dream, her hands grasp, dark against brilliant sheets. Her fingers never stop their reaching.

She crawls through the dream toward a distance voice that begs to be heard. A weary voice, alive and calling for a long time. So long, in fact, that she no longer recognizes the voice as her own.

Her cat, on the sill, watches her hands, then looks back out the window. Toward the sky. When the moon comes closer, he will gather it inside his paw.

32.
White Cats
William Doreski

In the Red Sox Room, shy white cats
scatter as I enter to empty
litter boxes and mop the floor.
Dirty dishes get washed and bleached.
Fresh water, canned food to share.
The white cats are deaf. They stare
pink-eyed out of their silent world.

They're afraid to let me stroke them,
shivering like foil at my touch.
No one will adopt them.   Their fear
crowds this small room where caged cats,
fierce and feral, sneer. I feed
the cages first, then place a tray
for the white cats on the floor.

A mass of sumac claws the window,
dims the room.   Some of these cats
have never set foot on solid earth.
Others have cowered in the weather
for years before being trapped
and brought here to domesticate.
The white cats, a single family,

arrived in a box on the stoop.
I want to pick them up and cuddle them,
but they'd mistake me for Cronus
eating his children.   The mop slurs
in the big plastic bucket.   The sumacs
droop clots of heavy red berries
and smear the window in the wind.

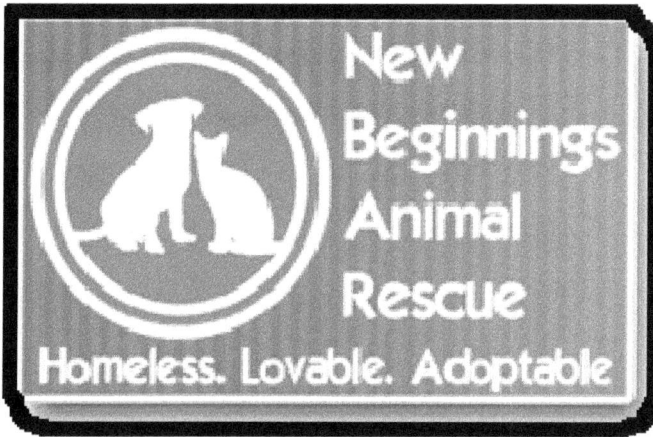

New Beginnings Animal Rescue (NBAR) was founded in 2010 to the overwhelming number of people who need help caring for or re-homing their companion animals. NBAR is run by a group of dedicated volunteers and fosters to make a difference in the lives of homeless animals. Our mission is to serve Southern Oakland County communities as a No-Kill rescue organization that finds suitable homes for indoor companion animals.

Contact Information:
New Beginnings Animal Rescue
2502 Rochester Road
Royal Oak, Michigan 48073
248-543-4070
http://nbarmichigan.org

www.ingramcontent.com/pod-product-compliance
Lightning Source LLC
Chambersburg PA
CBHW060804050426
42449CB00008B/1524